D0871598

Hogarth *The Complete Engravings*

Joseph Burke and Colin Caldwell

Hogarth

The Complete Engravings

Thames and Hudson · London

Published in France under the title
Hogarth Gravures
by Arts et Metiers, Paris

First published in Great Britain 1968

Illustrations printed in France, text printed in Great Britain by R. & R. Clark, Ltd, Edinburgh

William Hogarth was born on 10 November 1697, the year in which the Peace of Ryswick was concluded between England and France. In all the seven wars between the Glorious Revolution, as a result of which the power of the king was decisively checked by that of Parliament, and the final defeat of Napoleon in 1815, France was either the principal enemy or in alliance with the enemies of England. Hogarth was to live through three of these conflicts, the War of the Spanish Succession (1702–13), the War of the Austrian Succession (1740–48) and the Seven Years War (1756–63). At Stowe, the seat of the Whig Lord Cobham in Buckinghamshire, the Temple of Concord and Victory celebrates the great aim of Whig foreign policy: imperial expansion at the expense of France. In this Temple the pedimental sculpture by Scheemakers showed the Four Quarters of the Globe bringing their fruits to Great Britain. Inside, the bas-relief medallions represented a selection from the famous battles of British history. Without exception, these were victories against the French. Defeats no less spectacular were omitted. It is scarcely surprising that a French visitor of liberal opinions should regard these scenes as 'honteux pour l'humanité' by perpetuating 'les haines nationales'. The same writer, like Voltaire before him, was in sympathy with the Whig struggle for political liberty, which the gardens at Stowe so richly commemorated. On the whole he thought the temples and monuments a delicious spectacle for those who loved humanity and were sensible of 'la gloire', and ranked them on these grounds as highly as 'le temple auguste de Westminster'.

A self-confident oligarchy of great landowners and their dependants controlled Parliament, and in the mood of elation that followed the accession of George I and the final repudiation of the Stuarts with their absolutist ambitions, the ruling class advertised its proud independence of monarchy by building country houses in the classical style, associated with the Senators of Rome, on their estates. By contrast with Paris after the accession of Louis XV, the town-houses built by the aristocracy in London were conspicuously modest. Only a handful of great size were built by noblemen in the eighteenth century. While the landowners were investing in their country estates, the mainstay of their political influence because of the votes that they commanded, and creating a summer playground in the former Roman spa of Bath, the vitality of industry and commerce flowed into the metropolis and the provincial cities and seaports. The newly rich merchants and tradesmen spent their wealth soberly on handsome houses, solid furnishings and fine silver. The prosperity of the middle class provided a rapidly expanding market for the art of the engraver, who also profited from the popular demand for topical and satirical prints. At the same time the overcrowding of the cities created appalling conditions for the poor. The statistics of mortality show that the unfortunate on the land were even worse off, but in the cities the sight of misery was inescapable. What can chiefly be said in favour of urban life is that prosperity was increasing, and that living conditions apart from housing were better than they had been in the seventeenth century.

For the first time in her history Great Britain was regarded by Continental observers as an *avant-garde* nation in the world of culture and ideas. Not only was the British constitution profoundly admired by liberal intellectuals, but also the British philosophers. The Palladian revival encouraged architects to study the monuments of Rome, and for a short time English Classicism was the most advanced in Europe. Alexander Pope in poetry and Samuel Richardson in the novel figure in the long list of English writers who were widely read in the original or in translation. *Le jardin anglais*, perhaps the most original contribution of England to the visual arts of Europe, became a true spearhead of romanticism. The encyclopedia of Ephraim Chambers, which was first published in 1728 and reached a sixth edition in

1750, promoted Utopian visions of the amelioration of society by an alliance of the arts, science and manufactures. It is well known that this publication stimulated the far greater *Encyclopédie* of Diderot and d'Alembert. Voltaire, after his humiliation by the lackeys of the Chevalier de Rohan-Chabot late in 1725, sought permission to leave his country to visit England, arrived in 1726 and remained for over two years. He was an ardent admirer of English institutions and political liberties, and on his return to France became their most influential propagandist on the Continent.

Paradoxically, the intellectual ties between France and England were exceptionally close during this period of rivalry for Continental and imperial power. 'I believe', wrote Voltaire in a letter to the Abbé le Blanc in 1738, 'that an Englishman who thoroughly knows France, and a Frenchman who thoroughly knows England, are both the better for that knowledge.' An historical rôle of England was to make its contribution to the revolutionary changes that were to take place on the Continent in the world of ideas. It is true that the vitality of this influence was comparatively short-lived, for in its later phases *l'anglomanie* was symptomatic of fashionable taste rather than of advanced free-thinking. Just as the *Encyclopédie* of Diderot was greater and more far-reaching than that of Chambers, so the centre of philosophy later moved from England to Germany. What is important in the present context is that this period of intellectual emancipation is the one to which Hogarth belongs. He was twenty-five years younger than Reynolds, twenty-seven than Gainsborough. The conventional linking of his name with theirs can be misleading, as the dates of their deaths, respectively 1764, 1792 and 1788, indicate. He is firmly lodged in the age of the Whigs, whereas Reynolds and Gainsborough attained the height of their reputation and prestige in the age of the Tories, who came decisively into power two years after the foundation of the Royal Academy, which Hogarth had earlier opposed, in 1768.

William Hogarth expressed in his art the new mood of national elation, the critical spirit of the self-confident bourgeoisie and the liberal humanitarianism of his age. He was the first native-born English painter to become famous on the Continent, at a time peculiarly favourable to the reception of English ideas among liberal critics. He was even to become a hero of the Enlightenment, of which he anticipates many attitudes. One reason for his popularity was that the genius of the age found its highest expression in wit elevated to the level of poetry by its intensity of humane feeling. From Molière to Voltaire, from Congreve through Swift and Pope to Fielding, the literature of wit was enriched on a scale unprecedented since antiquity. The great comic writers of the second half of the century were bred in this school, which exposed folly, scarified pretension and lashed hypocrisy and cruelty. Its emancipating influence was transmitted through the age of romanticism by writers of the stature of Byron, Heine and Baudelaire.

It was the great and single-handed achievement of Hogarth to establish comedy as a category in art to be rated as highly as comedy in literature. There had been marvellous comic painters before him, but they were stigmatized as belonging to an inferior category, like the Dutch painters of low life. According to the hierarchy of artistic categories that was inherited from the Renaissance, *istoria* – the narrative depiction of elevated themes, especially from the Bible and antiquity – was the highest branch of art measured by a scale which placed low-life *genre* at the bottom. Whereas the Old Masters were chiefly renowned for their work as history painters, the painters of comic scenes were inseparably linked with *genre*. The case for the lower status of comic art was succinctly put by Sir Joshua Reynolds in his Third

Discourse (1770), delivered six years after the death of Hogarth:

> The painters who have applied themselves more particularly to low and vulgar characters, and who express with precision the various shades of passion, as they are exhibited by vulgar minds, such as we see in the works of Hogarth, deserve great praise; but as their genius has been employed on low and confined subjects, the praise which we give must be as limited as its object. The merry-making or quarrelling of the Boors of Teniers; the same sort of productions of Brouwer or Ostade, are excellent in their kind; and the excellence and its praise will be in proportion, as, in those limited subjects, they introduce more or less of the expression of those passions, as they appear in general and more enlarged nature.

Hogarth was acutely sensitive to the categorical depreciation of comic art, and with his friend Henry Fielding set about a campaign to raise its standing. The verdict of Reynolds, who was the declared champion of orthodoxy, shows that Hogarth did not convert the conservatives in his own profession. But at the conclusion of his discussion of comic art and other subordinate categories, Reynolds at least conceded the justice of the comparison with literature:

> All these painters have, in general, the same right, in different degrees, to the name of a painter, which a satirist, an epigrammatist, a sonneteer, a writer of pastorals, or descriptive poetry, has to that of poet.

The age itself was conscious that its true genius was for wit. When Garrick was planning his farewell performance on the stage, he first decided to appear in a tragic rôle. At the last moment he changed his mind, and substituted a comic one. Many years before, Reynolds had unconsciously forecast this decision in a painting which is at once a judgment of Garrick and a symbolic verdict on his age. In *Garrick between Tragedy and Comedy* (1761) the painter borrowed his composition from two Old Master paintings depicting the *Judgment of Hercules between Vice and Virtue*. The figure of Tragedy is borrowed from the Virtue of Guido Reni, Comedy from the Vice of Correggio. The actor is shown humorously apologizing to Tragedy, who points upwards to the heavens, while he is led away on the downward path by Comedy. By the wit of his allusions Reynolds showed that he thought Tragedy a higher form of art than Comedy. Both the gesture and expression of Garrick marvellously capture his spell-binding vivacity, and record for posterity that his deepest inclinations coincided with his essential gifts.

In a number of works and statements Hogarth identified his cause with comic literature. In the full-length self-portrait of *c.* 1757 the artist shows himself painting the Muse of Comedy. In *Masquerades and Operas* the works of Shakespeare, Ben Jonson, Dryden, Otway and Congreve are opposed to the importations of connoisseurship. In his self-portrait of 1745 the oval canvas rests on the works of Shakespeare, Milton and Swift. Congreve appears in the same list as Shakespeare, Swift alongside Milton. This is the key to his meaning. It is not sufficient to explain the invocation of great literary names simply by his ardent nationalism. It is true England could produce no genius of comparable eminence with Shakespeare, to be opposed to Raphael in painting. But Shakespeare was great in comedy as well as tragedy. Thalia and Melpomene were sisters of equal beauty. Congreve, who wrote the *Way of the World* under the inspiration of the former, had every right to stand on Parnassus with Dryden, who wrote *All for Love* under the inspiration of the latter.

Because his reasons for invoking literature were misunderstood, Hogarth exposed himself to the charge of being a 'literary' artist. The legend of the literary painter who was indifferent to composition or showed, in the words of Roger Fry, 'an extraordinary want of feeling' for formal relations can be traced back to his own age. Horace Walpole considered him 'rather as a writer of comedy with a pencil, than a painter'. He thought little of his painting, and asserted that his colouring and drawing rendered him unequal to an art which called for dignity and grace The comparisons that Walpole made in his encomium were solely with writers, a passing allusion to the bandits of Salvator Rosa excepted. He invoked the names of Molière, Congreve, Samuel Butler, Rabelais and Swift:

> If catching the manners and follies of an age *living as they rise*, if general satire on vices, and ridicules familiarised by strokes of nature and heightened by wit, and the whole animated by proper and just expressions of the passions, be comedy, Hogarth composed comedies as much as Molière: in his Marriage-à-la-mode there is even an intrigue carried on through the piece. He is more true to character than Congreve. . . . He smiled like Socrates, that men might not be offended by his lectures, and might learn to laugh at their own follies.

Other contemporaries likened him to Juvenal, and in 1816 the Reverend E. Ferrers published *Clavis Hogarthiana*, in which the works of Hogarth were wittily illustrated by quotations from 'Authors he never read, and could not understand', *i.e.* Greek and Latin writers.

'Other pictures we look at', wrote Charles Lamb, 'his prints we read.' Quite independently Baudelaire made the same point more critically when he referred to the profusion of details which could be sometimes confusing 'for the spectator – I was just about to say, for the *reader*'. Few artists have been read with greater admiration by famous writers. In his own lifetime Hogarth received the tributes of Swift, Fielding and Smollett. Hazlitt and Thackeray included him among their heroes of comedy. In Germany he was praised by Kant, Lessing, Lichtenberg and Goethe. An entire anthology of appreciation could be compiled from the criticism of French men of letters, commencing with Diderot. Such praise has done much for the reputation of Hogarth, but its literary source has diverted attention from his merits as an artist.

English aesthetes have always had a puritanical dislike of wit in art. Rowlandson, Gillray and Cruikshank can be safely praised, because they have little pretensions to be more than caricaturists. In no other country in Europe have the freedom and right of the artist to attain to the imaginative scope of literature been so vehemently attacked as in England by Roger Fry and Clive Bell. They abused 'literary' art, and chose their examples not from Giotto, Raphael and Poussin, but from the very worst nineteenth-century academic painters they could find. Their formal values were predominantly classical, and did not include the kinetic. Fry did not understand the formal theories that Hogarth propounded so clearly in *The Analysis of Beauty*, and totally disregarded his thesis that the formal values of comedy must be considered as carefully as those of a serious art. To those with puritanical notions of high art, an aesthetic of comedy is a contradiction in terms.

Other reasons can be adduced why the merits of Hogarth *as an artist*, as distinct from a comic genius whose medium of expression happened to be visual, have been more sympathetically discussed on the Continent than by the leading arbiters of taste in England. The rococo was never wholly assimilated in England, where it flourished chiefly under the two disguises of the Gothic and Chinese Tastes. Moreover, the rococo itself is not a favourite style with the puritanical aesthete. Some of the blame for aesthetic depreciation must be placed squarely on the shoulders of Hogarth himself. He seems to have felt a *Schadenfreude* in being misunderstood, and to have permitted and even encouraged an image which mystified his critics. On a memorable occasion he remarked to Mrs Piozzi apropos of the connoisseurs, 'Because I hate *them*, they think I hate *Titian* – and let them!' He outraged Horace Walpole by saying that he could paint a portrait as well as van Dyck. In print after print he attacked the connoisseurs for their patronage of ancient marbles, Old Masters and foreign art generally. He compared nature with art, to the disadvantage of the latter.

If his statements are examined carefully, it becomes apparent that he did not attack foreign art as such, that he passionately admired the Old Masters and that he took his principal standards of exellence from classical sculpture. The French and Italian modes of art that he attacked were principally the performing ones: masquerade, pantomime and opera. He lampooned the connoisseurs for buying second-rate Old Masters and fake antiques, a very different thing from deprecating the masterpieces of the Renaissance and antiquity. Horace Walpole may have thought that Hogarth was running down van Dyck, because the statement that he reported was made in deliberately provocative language. But there is nothing in the statement itself which is critical of van Dyck. On the contrary, Hogarth had chosen the anglicized Fleming for his national hero in art, and hung his carved portrait outside his house as a manifesto of his admiration, the famous *Golden Head* of van Dyck familiar to all who frequented Leicester Fields. In Plate I of *The Analysis of Beauty* he assembled the masterpieces of Graeco-Roman sculpture known to his age, and used them to demonstrate his theories about the first-rate in art. So far from saying that nature was superior to art, he merely asserted that neither the ancients nor the moderns had 'ever yet come up to the utmost beauty of nature', a modest admission to which no artist need object. In another passage he confined his praise of nature to parts, a notion which has impeccable classical authority in the story of Zeuxis. There would have been no inconsistency if he had added to his statement about Titian to Mrs Piozzi, 'Because I hate *nature-menders*, they think I hate art – and let them!'

It is not the intention of this explanation to overstate the case for Hogarth as an artist, but merely to draw attention to the importance of considering his art in relation to its aesthetic intention and especially his own statements about formal values. The autobiographical writings and *obiter dicta* of Hogarth have often been quoted, but seldom with reference to his most important and original contribution to artistic theory, his aesthetic of comedy. The following account is based on these writings, supplemented by documentary records, notably the note-books of George Vertue, who collected materials for the history of the art of his own time in England as well as the past. Told in this way, the story of the life of Hogarth serves as an admirable introduction to his art, because the autobiography that he planned but never completed deals almost entirely with the experiences that shaped his evolution as an artist and determined the distinctive character of his work. He made several drafts, the first for inclusion in *The Analysis of Beauty* but later rejected from the final text, and the others for an *apologia* on which he was still working in the last years of his life. He followed the same method that he used in writing his treatise on aesthetics, namely, to begin with a short account and expand it later. It is the method of an artist who makes several sketches before elaborating the final version, and the great advantage for posterity is that he covered at least summarily the whole ground, so that we know his own verdict on his life although he left his manuscripts in such a muddle.

Hogarth begins the story of his life and artistic evolution by saying that he was born in the City of London. Peter Quennell, who has written the classic account of London as mirrored in the art of Hogarth in *Hogarth's Progress* (1955) – indeed an apter title for the perceptive monograph would have been 'Hogarth's London' – quotes the statement of Walter Bagehot about Dickens, that he 'described London like a special correspondent for posterity'. Like Dickens, Hogarth was a master of topography for whom places were the scenes in which the drama of life was acted. London was his stage, and he seldom departed from it. It is worthy of note that he did not specify the place in the City where he was born: Bartholomew Close, West Smithfield, a narrow court of tall houses nestling under the shadow of a medieval church and close to a fair-ground, a market place, a hospital and what was then the most cramped and sinister of the prisons of London, Newgate Gaol. He does not mention this, because like a true Londoner, he thought of himself as belonging to the city as a whole.

The population of London, at most a quarter of a million at the beginning of the seventeenth century, did not grow substantially in the eighteenth. In 1700 'it was something less than three-quarters of a million; in 1801, when the first Census was taken, somewhat over 850,000'. Mr John Hayes, from whose account I quote, notes that the wealth of the city and the value of its trade increased enormously, and that there was a fever of building. Hogarth saw the development of the Burlington and Grosvenor Estates in the West End, with their legacy of handsome squares and terraces, and new buildings figure as prominently as old ones in his prints. The aristocracy and middle classes chiefly benefited from the development, and the relatively static size of the population indicates a terrible mortality due to overcrowding and its concomitant diseases amongst the poor.

His father was a struggling author, whose 'dependence was chiefly on his pen'. For some years Richard Hogarth laboured at compiling a Latin Dictionary, but was cruelly treated by booksellers and printers. He died while his son was still an apprentice, and Hogarth attributed this early death partly to his failure to find a publisher, partly to his being 'disappointed by great men's promises'. Among the papers that the son preserved were letters from acquaintances who belonged to 'the first class' of society.

The only recorded publications of any substance by Hogarth's father are both texts for schools: *Thesaurum Trilingue Publicum: Being an Introduction to English, Latin and Greek* (London 1689) and *Disputationes Grammaticales* (1712). The other work he did for booksellers is unknown. In an age of classical learning, in which lexicographers were especially honoured, Richard Hogarth may have nursed hopes of fame and financial reward for his undertaking. The phrase recorded by the artist, 'great men's promises', can only refer to the payment or guarantee of subscriptions in advance, without which few publishers would embark on so costly a venture. It was a common practice for noblemen or other 'great men' to take out several subscriptions on behalf of a protégé, and to obtain others from their friends. Dr Johnson later waited unsuccessfully on Lord Chesterfield for a similar favour. Before dying so bitterly disappointed, Hogarth *père* may well have inculcated in his son something of his own feeling of resentment towards patrons who encouraged hopes only to dash them.

There is a good reason for believing this to be true. The statements made by Hogarth about his life are highly selective, and the principle of selection was to choose what he regarded as significant for his career and evolution as an artist. Just as he regarded it as important to record that he was born in the City of London, but did not give the precise location, so he does not mention that his father kept a private school in Ship Court, Old Bailey, and that he had previously conducted another school of his own in his native county of Westmorland. This was probably the main source of his livelihood, rather than authorship. Neither of these facts was added when the artist elaborated his first draft. It is always 'the affair of the dictionary', 'the failure of the dictionary', 'the disappointment by great men's promises', to which he recurs. The last phrase might be applied to one aspect of his life-work as a satirist. Patrons were always a favourite target of attack, and the cause of the independent artist was one he never let die.

Richard Hogarth may also have told his son that he had a literary great-uncle, Thomas 'Hoggart', a farmer of Westmorland who wrote rustic comedies and satires in the vernacular of North Country farmers and peasants. The *Remnants of Rhyme* by Thomas Hoggart, who spelt the name of Hogarth as it was pronounced, was not published until 1855, but if the artist heard satirical passages quoted and humorous scenes described, his mind would have been early attuned to the comedy of low life.

The son of the schoolmaster was not, by his own admission, a model pupil. In later life he quoted Greek and Latin authors, but misspellings, like *fronta nulla fides* for *fronti nulla fides* – a warning not to trust appearances particularly applicable to patrons – suggest that these were scraps he picked up by ear. In his account of his childhood the artist introduced another central or recurrent theme of his auto-biography, his love of amusements. Again he selects only those amusements that were significant for his art. These were three: spectacles, mimicry and drawing. He had 'a naturally good eye', and 'shows of all sorts' gave him uncommon pleasure when he was still an infant. Mimicry, 'common to all children, was remarkable in me'. Finally, he became obsessed with drawing after early visits to a neighbouring painter whose name he does not record. A possible candidate is William Wollaston (1660–1724), whom Hogarth quotes in this section of his life. He was later to find an early patron among his kinsmen. He was also stimulated by friends at school who shared his enthusiasm for drawing. When he wrote out his school exercises he began the practice of decorating them with 'ornaments'. Blockheads with better memories beat him when the exercises were marked, but his ornaments were 'particularly distinguished'.

A precocious love of drawing is common to nearly all artists. More revealing are the statements about spectacles and mimicry. The spectacles that he would have seen as a child, the Lord Mayor's procession and Saint Bartholomew's Fair, with its booths, side-shows and theatrical performances, later provided him with a rich source of material. The child so enamoured of spectacles may well have been taken across the river to see Southwark Fair, the subject of one of his most memorable engravings. He also depicted public executions. Let us hope his humane parents kept him away from these as an infant, although he was in little more than toddling distance of Newgate Gaol. But he would not have been a normal schoolboy if he had avoided the terrible scenes, and in any case this would have been difficult, as the school kept by his father was even closer to the prison than his home. In the public executions that provided a Roman holiday for Londoners the antics of the crowd provided the amusement, the sufferings of the victim occasioned pity and terror. This was close to the formula of tragi-comedy that the artist later exploited in his satires.

The statement about mimicry is perhaps the most significant of all. The mimic feels himself into the characters and attitudes of his targets. He is also naturally attracted to the theatre, which in fact became the recreational passion of the artist. *The Analysis of Beauty* is one of the earliest treatises on aesthetics to develop the notion of empathy, basic to his aesthetic of comedy and its formal values. In looking at the characters portrayed by Hogarth, their expressions and gestures, it is profitable to recall that he not only observed momentary contortions of the face and expressive attitudes in daily life, but mimicked them.

On 2 February 1713–14, the Registry of Apprentices of the Merchant Tailors Company records his apprenticeship to Ellis Gamble, a goldsmith and engraver on silverplate, who sold both plate and jewellery at his shop in Cranbourne Alley, Leicester Fields, for a term of seven years. He tells us that he was taken early from school, and because Gamble did not become a freeman of the Merchant Tailors Company with the right to take apprentices until 1713, it is possible that he began his training even earlier. In his account of his apprenticeship Hogarth makes it clear that he was extremely dissatisfied with the method of training. Both in the *Analysis* and his autobiographical manuscripts he rides a favourite hobby-horse, the futility of copying. The copyist, he drives home with every emphasis at his command, never learns. French readers must be warned against identifying the training of an *ornémaniste* in Paris with that of an engraver on silverplate in London. The status of the French *ornémaniste* was much higher. Some became famous painters and even architects, and most were well taught to draw by their masters. There is no evidence that Hogarth was ever taught to draw from the model or nature as an apprentice. He learned to handle the tools of his craft, and he was set to copy. As a craftsman he imitated exclusively art, never nature. The bulk of his work was decorative, with a strong bias to heraldic ornament. He copied or adapted allegorical figures and their emblems. The highest he could aspire to in his craft was book illustration, at a time when it was the discreditable practice of some London book-sellers to pirate French and other Continental designs and publish them under the name of the engraver who copied them. In other cases the engraver reproduced designs supplied by well-known English painters. More rarely, he worked from drawings of his own invention.

Such was the dislike that Hogarth developed for copying, and so little the progress that he felt he was making, that he described the whole of the time he spent as an apprentice as largely wasted. This is one of the few of his statements with which it is tempting to disagree, or at least state a reservation. In addition to copying it was necessary to learn how to adapt, in other words, to make more or less inventive use of artistic sources. In doing so he was stocking his mind with images, although he complained that the impressions were weak and readily effaced. Another reiterated complaint was that he was not thinking while he was copying. However this may be, he gained from his experience at least one advantage that he later turned to good account. He was firmly grounded in a style which he became adept at parodying, the baroque. He was also introduced to the emerging style of the French rococo. He was, so to speak, on the ground floor of the new style, which partially accounts for his later susceptibility to the influence of French rococo painting. The London goldsmiths, many of whom were Huguenots, kept in close touch with Parisian innovations. The shopcard of Ellis Gamble, which Hogarth designed later, advertised his wares in both English and French. The artist who was to pick up so much from Mercier, Gravelot and the sculptor Roubiliac was not brought up in a wholly insular tradition, even at the outset of his craft training.

Hogarth admired fine work, but with extraordinary candour he tells us that he was too fond of his pleasures and too impatient by nature to attain 'that beautiful stroke on copper' which other artists acquired by early habits of industry and by taking great pains. It was during this period of dissatisfaction with the drudgery of his craft that he formed the ambition to escape from it by becoming a painter. As a boy his imagination was fired by seeing the monochrome paintings of Sir James Thornhill in the cupola of St Paul's Cathedral and the more ambitious and splendidly coloured decorations at Greenwich. Thornhill probably began work at Greenwich late in 1708, finishing the Lower Hall in 1714 and the Upper Hall *c.* 1725. The paintings in progress kept 'running in my head', so that he determined to continue with engraving only so long as necessity compelled him.

In addition to these magnificent commissions of church and state, Thornhill was employed by many of the aristocracy to decorate their great houses with history paintings. The spectacle of a native artist wholly relieved from the drudgery of portrait painting to adorn churches and princely buildings with grandiose allegorical and elevated subjects from the Bible and classical mythology was to haunt the imagination of English painters throughout the century. In the case of Hogarth the impact was decisive. He was well aware that van Dyck was the greater artist. But van Dyck, as the favourite painter of Charles I, was principally employed in painting portraits, whereas Thornhill was the first Court Painter both to be born an Englishman and to be given a whole series of commissions comparable in thematic scope and splendour of architectural setting with the greatest undertakings of the Old Masters. Might not his example be followed by others, and English art under the Georges attain to heights as glorious as those of Renaissance art under Italian popes and princes?

More sophisticated intellects than that of the boy-apprentice had delusively entertained the same patriotic hopes. In 1710 the Earl of Shaftesbury publicly appealed to statesmen and nobles to facilitate 'this happy Birth, of which I have ventured to speak in a prophetic style'. His cry for an English renaissance of the arts was taken up by many writers. It is easy to ridicule these patriotic ambitions, which were so uncritically supported that the mediocre William Kent could be acclaimed as the English Raphael, just as Benjamin West was later dubbed the American one. But in the case of Hogarth there was some excuse for the enthusiasm with which he viewed the work of Thornhill. He had not made the Grand Tour, and had no adequate standards for comparison. He knew the Old Masters only from reproduction in prints. The vitality of paint and colour was missing in these, and the vast colouristic machines of Thornhill, who was not without talent, constituted an Indian Summer of the baroque in England which may still be studied with interest and qualified admiration by the devotees of the European movement.

Henceforth the ambitious apprentice had two careers simultaneously in view. The first and more pressing was to make his way as an engraver. The second was to follow in the path of Thornhill. The surprising fact is that he achieved success in both of them, although with delay and some difficulty in the second. He was to execute more history paintings on a grandiose scale for churches and public buildings than Sir Joshua Reynolds, who as President of the Royal Academy guided that institution to become a training-ground for a national school of history painters. Hogarth decorated the Grand Staircase of St Bartholomew's Hospital with the *Good Samaritan* and *Pool of Bethesda*; *Paul before Felix* still dominates the Hall of Lincoln's Inn; in the Court Room of the Foundling Hospital *Moses Brought to Pharaoh's Daughter* occupied a whole compartment; and the price he received for the great triptych of the *Ascension* for St Mary Redcliffe, Bristol, five hundred guineas, was, he claimed, a record for the time. In 1757, at the age of sixty, he succeeded the son of Thornhill as Sergeant-Painter to the King. The highest ambition of a painter was to become the first painter of a Court. Hogarth achieved this, in title if not in practice.

In many other respects his career parallels that of his boyhood hero. Thornhill as leader of his profession had conducted a private academy. Hogarth secured control of the St Martin's Lane Academy, which for a memorable period in its history was known as Hogarth's Academy. His house in Leicester

Fields, opposite the one later occupied by Sir Joshua Reynolds, was as handsome and fashionably situated as that of Thornhill in Covent Garden. He kept a coach and six servants, and maintained a country retreat at Chiswick. It must be admitted that he did not, like Thornhill, become a member of Parliament with a country estate, and he was never knighted, possibly because he had offended George II by an indiscreet satire on the royal guards. Nor was he able to devote himself exclusively to history painting. With these exceptions he became the true heir of Thornhill, whose daughter he married.

Posterity is less interested in the career of the Sergeant-Painter than the one that opened out of his work as an engraver. In April 1720 he published a shopcard with his name flanked by the figures of History and Art, and with the address of the last house occupied by his father in Long Lane adjoining Smithfield Market. It is not known how the family managed to support itself in the two years following his father's death in 1718. The *Shopcard of Mary and Anne Hogarth* (1730) notifies a change of address from the corner of Long Walk, and it is possible that the widow started the frock shop there. In any case the family became independent by going into trade. It was a remarkable feat of enterprise for the family of a classical scholar, and underlies the later attitude of Hogarth to patronage. He had achieved independence before he ever sought a patron. He had already made his livelihood, and could state his own terms. Reynolds never forgot the debt he owed to his West-Country patrons, and even Gainsborough, who was less of a courtier, kept in touch with some of the Suffolk gentry who had commissioned portraits and recommended him to their friends. Hogarth was conscious of no such obligation.

In his first period from 1720 to 1728 Hogarth earned his living entirely as an engraver. He devoted more space to this period of his life in his autobiographical writings than to any other, for during it he became an artist as distinct from a craftsman. His first step was to join the newly founded St Martin's Lane Academy in 1720, the year of his freedom. In the Great Room he was able to draw from the antique and from life in the company of older painters as well as students. The joint managers were Johan van der Bank and Louis Chéron, both practitioners of the late baroque. A few years later, in 1724, he transferred to the Academy of Sir James Thornhill in Covent Garden. Why he did not do so in the first instance is obscure. The private or subscription academies of the time were not merely schools, they were also attended by established artists for fellowship and discussion, and to save the expense of hiring their own models. It would have been natural for the craftsman to wish to present himself to his hero after he had gained some proficiency in his academic studies. However this may be, his painting technique is sufficiently close to the manner of Thornhill to warrant the assumption that the latter was his principal master in oils.

The central topic to which he gave so much space was his self-education by the use of a mnemonic system. In his attendance at the Academy he noted the time and the labour necessary to make progress, and set his mind to the task of discovering 'a shorter way'. He evolved a technical memory, so that 'when I was at my pleasures, I could be at my studies'. The *memoria technica* that Hogarth used has never been satisfactorily explained. He tells us that it was his own invention, and that it was inspired by his dislike of copying. The same objection applied to drawing from the life as to copying from engravings: 'as the eye is often taken off the original to draw a bit at a time, it is possible to know no more of the original when the drawing is finished than before it was begun'. His 'short way' was to get objects by heart. Instead of copying, he wished to 'read the language of objects', and if possible find 'a grammar' to this language. He started to collect materials from what he saw, retain them in his memory and test upon the canvas how far he was advancing. He discovered that 'a coarse bold stroke or brush' could convey action and expression more truly and distinctly than 'the most delicate finishing', which could actually be 'a fault' in engraving. Much to his satisfaction, he became skilled in catching 'momentary actions and expressions'.

He describes his *memoria technica* as a form of shorthand, by which he retained objects *lineally* in his mind. He repeated mentally the parts of which objects were composed, and found that he could afterwards reconstruct them on paper 'without drawing on the spot'. He does not use the term *memoria technica* or *ars memorativa*, but 'technical memory', a literal translation of the former too close to be coincidental. The most likely source of his information about the systems of antiquity is his father, who after all was a classical grammarian. Common to the ones described by both Cicero and Quintilian is their visual framework. In his *De Oratore* Cicero describes the legendary invention of the *ars memorativa* by Simonides. The story is one which must have appealed strongly to the scholar who spoke so bitterly to his son about great men breaking their promises. Scopas, a nobleman of Thessaly, had commissioned Simonides to write a panegyric for a fixed sum. When the panegyric was read at a banquet, the patron noted that a passage had been inserted in praise of Castor and Pollux. He accordingly told the poet that he would pay only half the sum agreed upon, and that he must apply to the twin gods for the other half. Two strangers sent a message to Simonides that they wished to see him outside the banqueting hall. He found no one there, but during his absence the roof of the hall collapsed, and Scopas and all his parasites were killed. Simonides, who now realized that the two strangers were the gods come to punish the infamous patron, was able to remember the places at which the dead had been sitting, and thus enabled their relatives to find the corpses:

> He inferred that persons desiring to train this faculty [of memory] must select places and form mental images of the things they wish to remember and store those images in the places, so that the order of the places will preserve the order of the things, and the images of the things will denote the things themselves, and we shall employ the places and images respectively as a wax writing-tablet and the letters written on it.

Hogarth did not use the visual framework of *loci* and *imagines*. Instead, he reduced objects to lines, S- and C-curves, and straight lines at angles. He gives an example of his mode of linear analysis in Figure 71 of Plate II of *The Analysis of Beauty*, in which each linear notation refers to a figure in the central scene of the Ball. He was right to describe his method as a personal invention. But that it was prompted by the systems of antiquity is suggested by the remarkable correspondences between his own description and those of Cicero and Quintilian, and especially the anonymous author of *Ad Herrenium*, at that time attributed to Cicero. He uses the same analogies with alphabet and grammar. Those who want to train their memory, he tells us, must have as their aim as perfect a facility as those who write by combining the letters of the alphabet. The artist must read the language of forms with the aid of a grammar. Notation must be supported by repetition. All these statements can be matched in the writings of classical rhetoricians.

The prodigious visual memory that Hogarth trained as a young man was exercised on art as well as on nature. Among the artists from whom the late Dr Antal has detected precise borrowings are Callot, the Dutch painters of *genre* (especially Jan Steen), Rembrandt, Brueghel, Bosch, Raphael and the

Carracci. The engraved reproduction was his access to the Old Masters, his substitute for the Grand Tour. His range was omnivorous, and included broadsheets and popular topical satires. Among English artists only William Blake rivals him in the avidity with which he studied prints, and the imaginative use he made of them. Because his mode of assimilation was mnemonic, he did not so much steal as absorb from the originals.

In this section of his autobiography he returns again to the subject of his pleasures. 'Be where I would', he writes, 'with my eyes open, I could have been at my studies, so that even my pleasures became a part of them, and sweetened the pursuit.' He is said to have frequented the Clare Market Actors Club, for which he later designed a ceremonial tankard, while still an apprentice. The club met in a tavern situated between Drury Lane and Lincoln's Inn Fields, and consisted chiefly of actors, authors and artists. The tavern itself was a favourite rendezvous of actors, and as such open to any stage-struck apprentice who could pay his bill. For the rest of his life he was to be associated with playwrights and actors, and he is known to have acted on at least one occasion with his friend Garrick in amateur theatricals.

The first steps of Hogarth in this period, 1720 to 1728, are nearly always imitative of art rather than nature. He played what Robert Louis Stevenson called 'the sedulous ape', imitating the manners of all and sundry who caught his fancy. He could not altogether free himself from the bad habits of the copyist, so much so that attribution, when it is not documented, presents special difficulties, for some of the early commentators were credulous collectors anxious to authenticate their holdings. Nevertheless, certain predilections and talents distinguish his identifiable early work from a mere pastiche of styles. His images are legible and striking. He is at his most inventive in comic scenes. The habit of abstract analysis that he had acquired by practising his mnemonic system helped him to make formal arrangements, particularly of geometrically shaped objects, which are remarkably advanced for the time.

His earliest engravings were commissioned by goldsmiths, tradesmen, booksellers and printsellers. In these cases the remuneration was agreed upon in advance. His first topical satires, *The South Sea Scheme* and the *Lottery*, both dated 1721 although the second may have been finished later, were sold at two addresses, Mrs Chilcot in Westminster Hall and R. Caldwell, printseller in Newgate Street. The sight of his profits going to a printseller did not appeal to Hogarth. Accordingly he decided to publish on 'my own account', having found 'the tribe of this set of people' no better than his father had left them when he died. His first independent venture was *Masquerades and Operas* (1724), ridiculing 'the taste of the town'. To promote its sale he published two advertisements. In the first he gave a list of printsellers who were selling the original prints. He added that the original prints could also be obtained from the shop of William Hogarth, who engraved them. At this shop, the Golden Ball in Little Newport Street, copies as well-made as those sold by the printsellers could be bought for a penny apiece, instead of a shilling.

In precisely three days time the second advertisement appeared. In this he stated that the first was a sham advertisement written by himself to draw attention to the frauds of the printsellers. In other words, the first statement about the printsellers selling originals for a shilling, and the artist selling copies for a penny was a deliberate mystification intended to bewilder the public until he cleared up the riddle.

For the rest of his life Hogarth continued to practise the art of deliberate mystification. In the *Analysis* he gave the reason in a passage describing the fascination of riddles: 'the active mind is ever bent to be employed'. What appears to be contradictory in his prints is never so in reality; the most obscure image or detail always has a meaning. He also continued to advertise. The advertisements of Hogarth in the press make a fascinating if complex study. Some are literary squibs, designed to discomfort the connoisseurs. Others embody some of his most characteristic ideas, and the longest might almost be described as short essays. Their style was without precedent, and a conservative critic like George Vertue did not hesitate to use such derogatory terms as 'a schemist' and 'impudence'. His goal was independence, and by advertising in the press he was able to cut out the middleman and sell directly to the public. Unfortunately he had no legal redress for piracy, and it rankled with him that the printsellers were free to make copies and sell them more cheaply.

In the following year he published *A Burlesque on the Altarpiece of William Kent at St Clement Danes* (1725), in which he exposed the favourite painter of the Earl of Burlington for the mediocrity of his ideas and the bungling incompetence of his draughtsmanship. The Burlingtonians were actively championing Kent in opposition to Thornhill, and had recently secured for him the commission to decorate the State Apartments at Kensington Palace, much to the mortification of the King's Sergeant-Painter, who had expected it as a right. Professor Charles Mitchell has suggested that the satire was a deliberate move to obtain the favour of Thornhill. In any event Hogarth must have been admitted to the family circle, for there he captured the heart of Jane, the daughter of his hero. The couple eloped and were married on 23 March 1729 in Old Paddington Church.

A year before, he had made his début as a painter with *A Scene from the Beggar's Opera* (1728), which closes his first period and begins the second from 1728 to 1732. Probably he had already begun to paint portraits, but none can be dated earlier with absolute certainty. In any case the candidates for an earlier date among his paintings are of minor importance. Vertue first noted his 'daily success' in painting conversation pieces after August 1729. This corroborates the account given by the artist himself: 'I married and turned painter of portraits and small conversation pieces, with great success'. Up to the age of nearly thirty, *i.e.*, 1727, he had maintained himself 'in the usual gaieties of life' by engraving, and he records with pride that he was always a punctual paymaster. Presumably he made his runaway marriage with Jane Thornhill when he felt confident of his powers as a painter, and believed that he could earn a higher income. No doubt the fact that he did so played its part in effecting a reconciliation with his father-in-law, with whom the couple returned to live in Covent Garden after a short period on their own. In *Industry and Idleness* Hogarth later illustrated the familiar story of the industrious apprentice who married his master's daughter. It was not without relevance to his own career.

In this second period he was almost wholly occupied with painting. His output of engravings for four years was minimal. The conversation piece with which he made his reputation was an innovation in England, an informal mode of portraiture for which his inventive gifts were well suited. Neither Vertue nor Walpole give much space to his early engravings, although both single out the large illustrations to *Hudibras* for honourable mention, and the former noted 'the fluent genius' of his caricatures. But Vertue waxes almost eloquent about the early group portraits, referring to their 'great spirit', 'lively invention' and 'an universal agreeableness'. He was astonished by the rapid progress the craftsman had made after drawing at the Academy and getting 'some little insight and instruction in oil colours'. He attributed his success to force of judgment, a quick and ready conception and an exact imitation of natural likeness. He makes no reference to the technical memory, to which the artist himself ascribed the speed of his advance. But both artist and critic are at one in emphasizing the breakaway from the imitation of art to the observation of nature.

The origins of the English conversation piece are to be found in the informal group portraiture of the Low Countries, on a small scale influenced by *genre* and on a large scale influenced by Rubens, and the informal group portraiture of France, influenced by the *fêtes galantes* and *fêtes champêtres* of Watteau, himself a follower of Rubens and van Dyck in his youth. The name itself was taken from the Italian *conversazione* in the sense of a party or intimate gathering for recreation. It may be defined as an informal portrait group, generally with small figures, in a familiar private and proprietary setting, with an emphasis on relaxation, a precise attention to costume and accessories and frequently some measure of playful invention. It is distinguished from its Continental counterparts by its stress on the proprietary. The circle of musicians is shown in *their* clubroom, the lady gives a tea-party in *her* parlour, the nobleman receives his children in *his* library, or takes his family fishing or kite-flying in *his* park, the naval captain gives a drinking party in *his* cabin. Sometimes the setting is generalized, as in the *fêtes champêtres* of Watteau or the group portraits of Longhi and Troost, in which a real room may have served as the model but is scarcely presented as a specially memorable interior to be identified with the pride of the owner in his possession. These are the exceptions that prove the rule, for the most notable conversation pieces of Hogarth (who established the category in England), Arthur Devis and Zoffany are depictions of particular places as well as people.

Hogarth established the category in vogue, as the account of Vertue makes clear, but did not invent it. The most important of his predecessors was Philip Mercier (1689–1760), son of a Huguenot tapestry designer who settled in London *c.* 1724–5 and became principal painter and librarian to Frederick, Prince of Wales. In 1725–6 he painted *Viscount Tyrconnel with Members of Family in the Grounds of Belton House*, in which the group is informally assembled around Miss Darrel on a swing, a favourite rococo motif with which Mercier would have been familiar as an engraver after Watteau and his contemporaries. The English patron wanted a portrait of his house as well as his family, and the mansion is accordingly shown in the background. If the painting is compared with a late and completely mature rococo masterpiece, the *Swing* of Fragonard in the Wallace Collection, London, it can be seen that the insistence on topography favoured a much more realistic treatment, thus opening the category to the influence of Dutch *genre*.

This excursion into the painting of Hogarth is necessary because the liberating influence of the rococo was as decisive for his engraving as for his painting. It was transmitted by engraving, painting and later sculpture, and reinforced by his involvement with the contemporary theatre, where he witnessed a naturalistic revolution in acting which dates from the *Beggar's Opera* (1728). Hogarth is not a strictly rococo artist, for the reason already noted – that English conditions favoured an amalgamation with realism. A fusion takes place, but in this fusion the rococo is the crucial ingredient, for it was the vehicle of playfulness *par excellence* and as such refined the literal traditions of Dutch humour and boisterousness.

Hogarth was not satisfied by his rapidly growing practice as a portrait painter. Horace Walpole thought his employment the most ill-suited imaginable to a man whose turn certainly was not flattery, and whose talent was not adapted to look on vanity without a sneer. 'I entertained some notions', the artist writes, 'of succeeding in the grand style of history painting, and painted the staircase at St Bartholomew's Hospital *gratis*.' The paintings were received with praise as well as criticism, but no commissions followed. He considered the reason for the failure, and decided that the only hope for the future lay in going back to the course he had followed before he became a painter, namely, of 'dealing with the public in general'. Provided he could 'strike the passions' in his painting, he could make engravings and out of many small sales make a large sum, thus 'securing my property to myself'. His mind turned to 'modern moral subjects, a field unbroken up in any country or any age'. He was writing after the event, but his claim to have struck out on a novel path was confirmed by many of his contemporaries, including George Vertue, Horace Walpole and Sir Joshua Reynolds. Of these three Reynolds was the most explicit. 'This admirable artist', he stated, 'had invented a new species of dramatic painting.'

The third period, 1732 to 1745, is dominated by the dramatic cycles, which are the most original contribution of Hogarth to European art. It begins with *The Harlot's Progress*, published in 1732. Vertue records how Hogarth stumbled on his new mode by a happy accident:

> The most remarkable subject of painting that captivated the minds of most people, persons of all ranks and conditions from the greatest quality to the meanest, was the story painted and designed by Mr Hogarth of the Harlot's Progress and the prints engraved by him and published.
>
> Amongst other designs of his in painting he began a small picture of a common harlot, supposed to dwell in Drury Lane, just rising about noon out of bed and at breakfast. . . . This whore's déshabillé, careless and a pretty countenance and air – this thought pleased many. Some advised him to make another to it as a pair, which he did. Then other thoughts increased and multiplied by his fruitful invention, till he made six different subjects which he painted so naturally, the thoughts, and so striking the expressions that it drew everybody to see them – which he proposing to engrave in six plates to print, at one guinea each a set, he had daily subscriptions came in, in fifty or a hundred pounds a week.

The pair of paintings on an erotic theme was a favourite commission in France during the heyday of the rococo. The narrative cycle has an unbroken history from antiquity. In recent years a number of scholars have investigated the sources of the 'invention' of Hogarth, notably Hilde Kurz and the late Frederick Antal. The nearest precedent is to be found in the work of Dutch painters of *genre* in the seventeenth century, notably Jan Steen and the Hals School in Haarlem, who depicted similar characters and situations in paintings of the Prodigal Son. The *Cérémonies et coûtumes religieuses* of Bernard Picart were rich in significant detail, *ce superflu, si nécessaire*, which gave the history of the manners of the age. Hilde Kurz has discovered remarkably close antecedents in seventeenth-century Italian cycles of popular engravings, such as the *Life and End of the Harlot* and the *Miserable End of Those who Follow Harlots*. When all these sources and affinities have been noted and studied, the overwhelming impression that remains is one of originality.

The artist himself pinpointed the nature of the original feature. 'My picture', he wrote, 'was my stage, and men and women my actors.' The idea of the story may have been suggested by Daniel Defoe, whose *Moll Flanders* had been published in 1722 and was still popular reading. But Hogarth did not follow the form of a novel. His principal characters were limited in number, and constitute a true *dramatis personae*. Each scene is the principal scene of an act, and as such prepares the way for the next.

The popular Italian prints of the seventeenth century had also originated in the performance of actors, but there was a world of difference between the popular productions from which Hogarth drew his models and a theatre which had evolved from the glories of the Elizabethan stage and had been enriched by the influence of Molière.

According to Walpole, every engraver set himself to copy the series, and thousands of imitations were dispersed all over the kingdom. The artist had achieved fame but not independence. With characteristic resource he applied for redress direct to Parliament. It was his first experience of organizing artists to act together in their own interest, always a task of exceptional difficulty. A petition was signed, and a Bill drafted with professional legal advice. In 1735 the Copyright Act was passed, and became justly known as Hogarth's Act. The prints of *The Rake's Progress* were held back until their sale was protected by the new Act, and the first success was confirmed by the second. This time the profits were all his own: to cite Walpole again, 'the curtain was now drawn aside, and his genius stood displayed in its full lustre'.

Marriage-à-la-Mode (1745) concludes the series in strictly dramatic form. If the trilogy of dramatic cycles is taken as a whole, it will be noted that there is a consistent advance in both construction and technique. Certain features remain constant. The characters and situations are invariably borrowed from the stage. Moll Hackabout in *The Harlot's Progress*, Tom Rakewell, his faithful mistress and hideous rich bride in *The Rake's Progress*, Viscount Squanderfield and Counsellor Silvertongue in *Marriage-à-la-Mode* stand for types of the bawd, rake, seduced servant, wealthy spinster, spendthrift and seducer familiar to every contemporary theatre-goer. The lover surprised in a bedroom, the flirtation or intrigue at the levée, the arrest for debt, the revel in a tavern, the duel scene, the death-bed dénouement were no less stock episodes, each presented with its appropriate props and accessories. A plot is unfolded and, as Walpole pointed out, a sub-plot or intrigue is even carried on through *Marriage-à-la-Mode*. Every action could readily be translated into stage directions and in fact each of the stories gave rise to stage performances. To take only one example, in the Duel Scene from *Marriage-à-la-Mode* the Watch break in through the door (backstage right); the lover escapes through the window (backstage left); the Countess (centre-stage left) kneels in classic or heroic profile while the Earl (centre-stage right) dies in an exquisite parody of the rococo serpentine line of grace. The front of the stage is lit by the fire, against the light of which the Earl has fought to defend his honour. Characteristically, the villain has chosen to fight with his back to the light, thus securing an unfair advantage over his passionate opponent. The theatrical features are constant, as has been noted, but they are handled with progressive mastery culminating in the last of the series.

Hogarth had one major advantage as a painter over the stage producer. He could be topographically accurate, and by making London his stage add the contemporary realism of place to that of manners. The action could be subtly supported by the significant detail of the setting, to an extent which is hardly practicable on the stage. He was thus enabled to display all the skills he had acquired as a painter of conversation pieces. The harlot is shown in two rooms, the first in the apartment in which she is kept by her rich protector, the second the one she occupies in Drury Lane after her dismissal. In the first case it is clear that the Jewish merchant owns the contents of the room as well as the mistress he has placed in it. The second, for all its squalor, as clearly belongs to the harlot. Throughout the three cycles the artist shows the same sure sense of the proprietary as a revelation of character. A particularly subtle example is the scene in which the Rake is arrested for debt in St James's Street, then as now famous for its clubs. But the pavement belongs to the boot-blacks. It is where the gamins keep their club, discuss politics and gamble, in emulation of their betters.

The dramatic cycles were greatly admired by Henry Fielding, who was both playwright and novelist. Either under the influence of Fielding, or more probably in collaboration, Hogarth evolved a new species of comic history painting, corresponding to the scope of the epic rather than that of the drama. Both made theoretical pronouncements which explain the difference between the dramatic cycles and the new species of comic history painting. The term 'comic history painter' seems to have been invented by Fielding, who used it in the Preface of *Joseph Andrews* (1742), where he paid a tribute to the painter. He began by explaining that 'the Epic, as well as the Drama, is divided into tragedy and comedy'. A comic romance, such as his own novel, was a comic epic poem in prose, 'its action more extended and comprehensive [than the drama], containing a much larger circle of incidents, and introducing a greater variety of characters.' It was this wider scope to which Hogarth next turned his mind. He had mastered the dramatic mode of comedy; he would now show that he could shine in the epic.

None of the series that follow this radical revision of his aims could be faithfully presented on the stage. The circle of incidents is too large, the variety of characters too profuse. *Industry and Idleness* (1747) follows in the main the form of the novel. Its action is so extended that we trace the careers of two apprentices through all the stages of life except old age. It is comprehensive enough to include a Lord Mayor's procession and an execution at Tyburn, and the supporting cast is enormous. Like Fielding, Hogarth introduces episodes that are taken straight from the theatre, but they are set against a crowded tapestry of life. Taken together, the later series constitute a true *comédie humaine*, and justify the claim of both writer and artist that their work required intellectual resources and technical skills comparable to those of the writers of epic and drama in the tragic mode.

The *Four Prints of an Election* (1755–58) is the supreme masterpiece of this period, his *tour de force* in mock-heroic baroque parody. It opens with a banqueting scene, which is in the crowded Venetian tradition but alludes to the *Last Supper*, from which one of the groups is borrowed. *Canvassing for Votes* is an open street scene with a riot in the distance. *Polling for Votes* substitutes an elevated booth for the temple approached by steps, as in paintings of *Christ before Pilate* and the *Presentation of the Virgin*. The *Chairing of the Members* is an elaborate parody of two types of baroque history painting, the battle piece and the *sacra conversazione*. The goose that flies over the head of the first elected Member (only the shadow of the second can be seen) is wittily taken from the *Battle of Arbela* by Pietro da Cortona, which Hogarth knew from the engraving. In the Old Master painting, however, it is a superb eagle that flaps its wings over the head of Alexander the Great. The group of the enthroned Member supported by chairmen and escorted by his admirers is similarly adapted from the enthroned Madonna attended by saints, the spiral composition being translated into a zig-zag in accordance with the central doctrine of the aesthetic of the ridiculous, propounded at such length in *The Analysis of Beauty*, that the forms of comic art must parody by inversion those of the sublime.

It is difficult to divide the last, longest and richest period of the artist's life from 1745 until his death in 1764 as precisely as the years of evolution from 1720 to 1745. In 1720 he came out of his apprenticeship; in 1728 he commenced painting; in 1732 he invented a new species of dramatic painting. In each case there was a clear demarcation which coincides with a stage of advance. By 1745, when he abandoned the strictly dramatic mode, he had run through the gamut of his styles and reached full maturity as a painter. Up to this date the outside influences can be readily detected. After the first period, when he laid the foundations of his iconographic range by a wide study of the print, the contemporary French influences are especially significant. Without exception they are biased towards the rococo, the most vital *avant-garde* style of his age. In his second period as a painter of conversation pieces he assimilated the style of Mercier into the post-Kneller tradition of English painting. In the third period of the dramatic cycles he received a renewed French stimulus from Hubert-François Gravelot (1699–1773), an artist who was far superior to Mercier and ranks as a true *petit-maître* of the rococo. Gravelot arrived in England in 1732 and became a moving spirit in the St Martin's Lane Academy after Hogarth reorganized it in 1735. His modish skill in drawing made him a popular and effective teacher, and his fine sensitive line, cult of the silhouette and observation of both the texture of materials and their cut and hang were quickly imitated by a number of English artists, including Hogarth, Highmore and Gainsborough. The figure of the Rake in the levée scene is particularly close to the costume studies that Gravelot designed and engraved.

Hogarth admired Quentin De La Tour and visited France in 1743. But surely the strongest of all French influences, and the one that principally accounts for the astonishing advance that he made in the 1740s, was that of the sculptor Louis-François Roubiliac. There is little in the early conversation pieces to prepare the spectator for the heights that he achieved in *The Graham Children* (1742) and *Mrs Elizabeth Salter* (1744). The influence of sculpture upon painting has frequently been demonstrated by historians of Renaissance art, but has scarcely been mentioned in the context of eighteenth-century English painting, apart from iconographical borrowings. The illusionism of Roubiliac was far superior to that of any painter in England, and moreover his style of modelling lent itself to translation from clay into pigment. In 1741 Vertue saw the terracotta bust of Hogarth by Roubiliac in the latter's studio. By this date the painter and sculptor were close associates. They had first come together in the project to decorate Vauxhall Gardens with works by living British artists, whether native-born or of foreign extraction. Hogarth had been the prime mover, and had thrown himself into the scheme with all the enthusiasm of one who believed that artists must exhibit their work publicly if they were to escape dependence on patrons. He similarly originated the idea of presenting works to the Foundling Hospital (1746), a landmark in the history of exhibitions in England, and again received the powerful support of the greatest sculptor of the century in England.

If the bust is compared with the painter's self-portrait of 1745, it will be seen that in both a double shadow below the eye emphasizes the loose texture of the skin; the light falls on the slightly rotund tip of the nose; and the shape of the eye is transformed from the conventional almond of the Kneller school into a more dynamic pattern in which the upper lid curves sharply down on the inside to meet the sweep from the lower one. These are typical schemata for Roubiliac in modelling the head, and now become typical for the painter, who seems to have immediately recognized their illusionistic superiority to the stylized conventions of the urbane Augustan mask.

As with the paintings, so with the engravings, the majority of the most famous ones being made from paintings. The figures are more amply modelled; the chiaroscuro plays over textures, not merely schematic surfaces; and the spatial framework is filled with atmosphere. The one change that his engraving does not mirror is the increasing impressionistic fluency of his brushwork, culminating in

The Shrimp Girl. This seems to have been an autonomous development, once his style had been liberated from the academic finish to which he had first trained himself.

Marriage-à-la-Mode both closes the third period and opens the final one, to which it belongs by the maturity of its style. This maturity can be dated from 1740, when Hogarth was spurred to exceptional efforts as a painter by the full-length portrait of Captain Thomas Coram, executed two years after Roubiliac had scored his first major success with the statue of Handel for Vauxhall Gardens. The paintings were apparently ready for engraving early in 1743, but the supposed existence of a set of rejected designs makes it possible that Hogarth was dissatisfied after his visit to Paris in that year and repainted the whole set. The engraving by other hands, L.G. Scotin, S.F. Ravenet and Bernard Baron, may have occasioned further delays. Their publication revealed to the widest public that the strides he had made in single and group portraits extended to his most inventive compositions.

There is one danger in relating the evolution of the engraver too closely to that of the painter. During his final phase he constantly retraced his own steps, that is, turned back to his own past for inspiration. He allowed no form in which he had excelled to lapse altogether: vignette, tail-piece, conversation piece, dramatic episode, polemical and personal satire – he resumed them all. This habit of reversion led him to take up types of print which did not lend themselves to a more painterly treatment, particularly in cases where he himself remained his own engraver and designed directly for engraving on plate without the intermediary of painting. The two most conspicuous examples come under the heading of small pieces – subscription-tickets, tail-pieces, *jeux d'esprit* – and modern moral subjects designed to reach the young of all classes, but especially the lowest, with whom he had become deeply involved as a Governor of the Foundling Hospital.

In the former category he had shown his gift for abstract design as early as 1724 in *Royalty, Episcopacy and Law*, the title by which *Some of the Principal Inhabitants of the Moon* became generally known. A naturalistic painterly style must by its nature come into conflict with the demands of abstraction, and in a number of instances he modified his own to revert to his original delight in juggling with geometric shapes and patterns. *Crowns, Mitres, Maces* (1754) and *The Five Orders of Periwigs as they were worn at the Coronation, measured Architectonically* (1761) are two late examples that show he had lost none of his inventive audacity in abstract composition. They are among the designs which appeal particularly to modern taste, the latter being almost surrealist in its fantasy. Indeed a well-chosen selection which included Figure 89 of Plate II of *The Analysis of Beauty* could appropriately figure in an anthology of precursors of the modern movement.

The modern moral subjects for 'the instruction of youth' are discussed at some length in the autobiographical drafts, where he draws attention to their exceptional character. Fine engraving, he tells us, was not necessary, because his aim was to be intelligible to the simplest minds. His priorities were 'character and expression'. Everything is designed to stress a single point, and he avoids the elaborate polyphony of forms that characterize his comic history paintings, and justify his description as the Poussin of the mock-heroic.

These self-imposed limitations seem to have brought out his highest powers as a graphic designer. Advance in naturalism and technique is not the same as artistic progress. Hogarth had early shown the gift of creating a compulsive image, and some of the scenes of *The Harlot's Progress* haunt the imagination with a power to which later and more sophisticated designs fail to attain. So in *Industry and Idleness*, the scenes in which the idle apprentice is sent to sea and shares a garret with a prostitute have a stark simplicity of design which attain that classic inevitability to which nothing can be added, and from which nothing can be taken away. The masterpiece of the category is *The Four Stages of Cruelty*. Because he had limited his aims and simplified his technique, the realization of his ideas and his technical resources were perfectly matched. In *The First Stage*, one of the most economical and admirably disposed of his compositions, the engraving has lost none of the clarity and vigour of the drawing, but seems rather to grow out of it.

Hogarth attached a special importance to his attack on cruelty. He declared that, speaking as a man not an artist, he would rather in his own mind be the author of this series than of the Raphael cartoons in Hampton Court. In a moving passage he expressed his horror of cruelty, 'the very describing of which gives pain'. He defended the strong manner in which he portrayed it as necessary to have an effect on 'the most strong hearts'. He speaks with the language of the heart, yet the horrific scenes are enlivened with the most masterly touches of wit. In the opening scene there is something indescribably comic about the unfortunate cat who is thrown out of a high attic and floats downwards tied to two balloons which act as wings agitated by its frantic struggle.

In giving his aim as 'the instruction of youth' Hogarth is true to his psychological obsession with the predicament of the young. He had himself surmounted the misfortunes and obstacles of his early life. His marriage was childless; perhaps he found some compensation in his work for the Foundling Hospital. He was more than a Foundation Governor who regularly attended meetings, more than a personal benefactor active in securing gifts. He and his wife took boys into their household, trained them and gave them a start in life. The central theme of his moral argument is social responsibility for the young. In the trilogy of dramatic cycles the wages of sin are death in the first and third, madness in the second. But his central characters are not simply the victims of their own depravity and folly. The sins of the fathers are visited on the children. In all three series the opening scene emphasizes the responsibility of the parent or, where parents are absent, the duty of those who stand *in loco parentis*. The country girl who becomes a harlot arrives in London with the present of a goose to 'her loving cousins in Thames Street'. But the loving cousins fail to meet her, and she is accosted by a bawd who poses as a rich and kindly woman anxious to help young girls. The seduction takes place under the eyes of a clergyman who has accompanied the wagon on his horse. He ignores the episode, for he is selfishly engrossed in a letter of recommendation to the Bishop of London. Lichtenberg was wrong to identify him as the father of the girl, but his mistake if anything points the moral, for it was the duty of the clergyman to act *in loco parentis* to the friendless girl. The rake is the victim of the neglect of his father, whose miserliness has already led him to embark on a course of deceit. In *Marriage-à-la-Mode* the dissolute spendthrift and his giddy bride are likewise sacrificed on the altar of parental selfishness. Thomas Idle in *Industry and Idleness* breaks the heart of his mother, who is a widow. The wilful boy lacks a father who might have been able to control him.

The moral may seem a simple one today, just as the virtues of industry and thrift that Hogarth inculcates may appear to have a somewhat Victorian flavour. To read the prints in this way, however, is to miss the whole point of his criticism of society. It is the responsibility of society for the young that is his target when he stresses that the selfishness of parents breeds folly and vice. His central message for the young is the doctrine of self-reliance. Hogarth is essentially a humanitarian, not a puritan moralist, and the man who wrote that the *Four Stages of Cruelty* were 'done in hopes of preventing in some degree that cruel treatment of animals which makes the streets of London more disagreeable to the human mind than anything whatever' had a sensibility to suffering and a concern for human dignity which gave his satires an intensity of feeling and conviction far transcending the boisterousness of Dutch *genre* and the coarseness of contemporary polemical caricature.

The Analysis of Beauty (1753) was written when he had the greater part of his achievement behind him. It is the first treatise in the history of European aesthetics to make formal values both its starting point and its central theme. In the course of his argument Hogarth finds fault with symmetry, frontalism, absolute uniformity, equalities and parallelisms, in short, all those formal devices by which the classical artist attained to his order or harmony of distinct parts. To the balanced equilibrium and harmonious resolutions of classic art he opposes the kinetic values of the dynamic baroque. For each classical principle that he attacks he substitutes its baroque opposite. None of the five concepts of antithesis between the Renaissance and baroque modes of perception formulated by Woelfflin escapes his attention. There are no lines in nature. He devotes a long passage to illusionistic recession. He advocates cutting into forms. The lesser parts merge into the bolder. Breadth of shade obliterates narrow distinctions, as when Windsor Castle is viewed at the rising or setting of the sun.

On his title-page he summed up his theory by depicting two emblems. The first is his supreme symbol of baroque beauty, the serpentine line. It is encased inside the classical form of a pyramid. Both this pyramid and the base on which it stands are shifted slightly to one side, so that the classical triangle is given a baroque twist. But the classical principle is observed, and this is characteristic of an artist who takes his stand on the side of the English compromise with the baroque. Wren is praised unreservedly, Rubens criticized for being too bold, swelling and S-like in his curves. He cites with approval the lines of Milton:

> Mystical dance! –
> – Mazes intricate,
>
> Eccentric, intervolv'd, yet regular
> When most irregular they seem.

Because irregularity conceals regularity, and even intricacy is composed, he is able to admire unreservedly the masterpieces of late antique sculpture. When he comes to the Old Masters of Italy, he looks for and finds his favourite principles, with a bias to Mannerism. Parmigianino, for all his incorrectness, displays 'an inexpressible greatness of taste'.

The ultimate criterion by which he justifies his formal *credo* is psychological. 'Pursuing is the business of our lives . . . every arising difficulty, that for a while attends and interrupts the pursuit, gives a sort of spring to the mind, enhances the pleasure, and makes what would else be toil and labour, sport and recreation.' In accordance with this psychological principle, he defined beauty as 'a composed intricacy of form, which leads the eye, and through the eye the mind, a kind of chase'. As a verbal formulation of the baroque style this could hardly be bettered. In a later passage he added an epithet to the formula: beautiful forms lead the eye 'a wanton kind of chase'. By adding this epithet, by which he meant not 'dissolute' but 'free and frolicsome', he extended the principle from the baroque to rococo.

The aesthetic of comedy takes the argument to a higher level than this brilliant rationalization of observed principles. Here he begins with the psychological principle, the pleasurable mental sensations that are provided by a playful surprise. Wit is the surprising juxtaposition of opposite ideas.

When improper, or incompatible excesses meet, they always excite laughter, more especially when the forms of those excesses are inelegant, that is, when they are composed of unvaried lines.

He gives as an example a contrivance he had seen at Bartholomew-Fair, which he illustrated in Figure 17 in Plate I of the *Analysis*. This contrivance, which he tells us 'always occasioned a roar of laughter', was a fat grown face of a man, with an infant's cap on and the child's dress so placed under the chin, as to seem to belong to the head.

Just as the ideas of the comic artist surprise by being the opposite of what the mind is led to expect, so do the forms. Comic art astonishes the eye by unexpected deviations from the norm, *i.e.*, the ideal and the heroic baroque. In both his analysis of beauty and his analysis of the ridiculous, Hogarth took as his norm or standard the dominant style of his age, which determined the mental set of formal expectations. By inversion and 'excess' comic art parodies baroque style as well as baroque iconography. This is a much more fundamental observation than anything in his analysis of the baroque style, for it is capable of application to all forms of comic art. The kinetic theory of which the serpentine line is the symbol fits Rubens, but not Mondrian. It excludes much classical art. But the formal values of the comic artist play by inversion and excess on those forms that the spectator is led to expect, whatever the norm for the age may be. The style to be parodied does not have to be baroque, although this was the one that Hogarth as the child of his age naturally chose.

It is basic to his argument that the inversion or exaggeration of ideal forms can never be applied by a mechanical formula. Comic form is essentially *expressive*. Of the many examples that he gives, one in particular, the analysis of the Italian Harlequinade, throws light on his own practice:

The attitudes of the harlequin are ingeniously composed of certain little, quick movements of the head, hands and feet, some of which shoot out as it were from the body in straight lines, or are twirled about in little circles.

Scaramouch is gravely absurd as the character is intended, in over-stretch'd tedious movements of unnatural lengths of lines. . . .

Pierrot's movements and attitudes, are chiefly in perpendiculars and parallels, so is his figure and dress.

Punchinello is droll by being the reverse of all elegance . . . his limbs are raised and let fall almost altogether at one time, in parallel directions, as if his seeming fewer joints than ordinary, were no better than the hinges of a door.

The form of the movements expresses the character in each case.

With two reservations, the artist practised what he preached. The first is that he applied his formal system, like the mnemonic one, more consistently to parts than the whole. Secondly, his imitation of life is always anchored to realism. Like the Dutch artists, his art occupies a middle ground between the literal rendering and one that is transformed by style.

Edgar Wind has defined the correct visual assumption to make in looking at his art as a regard for kinetic intricacy, ideally suited for a strict mode of anecdotal painting. Julius Meier-Graefe, who, despite some partisan exaggerations, wrote what is still the best account of his style, made a related observation after stressing the affinities with the rococo and the essential rôle of visual movement:

> Minuteness of observation was proper to Hogarth, as was also minuteness of material. The idea of the picture grew from the sum of single observations, which he was able to seize and co-ordinate.

Read kinetically from part to part, his satirical prints lead the eye, and through the eye, the mind, a wanton kind of chase, just as much as the baroque compositions that they formally parody by inversion and excess.

At the time of his death Hogarth had an extraordinarily varied record of original achievement behind him: history paintings, the sole category in which he could consistently apply the forms of beauty that he expounded in the *Analysis*; conversation pieces; the dramatic cycles; the comic history paintings in an epic mode; and a range of satire so wide that it is impossible to do justice to it in a general account. In his struggle to emancipate the artist from dependence on patronage he had promoted public exhibitions of contemporary British art at Vauxhall Gardens, the Foundling Hospital and the Society of Artists; secured the Copyright Act; and supported the St Martin's Lane Academy in opposition to schemes to found a Royal Academy. He had become Sergeant-Painter to two kings who otherwise failed to patronize him, but at least recognized his leadership of the profession. He had fought hard for the humanitarian causes of his age. Appropriately he closed his independent *œuvre*, as he had begun it, with a satire on connoisseurship, *The Bathos* (1764), on which he was still working at the time of his death. The legend reads:

> FINIS, or the Tail-Piece. The Bathos, or manner of sinking in Sublime Painting, inscribed to the Dealers in Dark Pictures.

Hogarth must have enjoyed his ideas as they crowded upon his imagination while he created a mock-rococo counterpart to Dürer's *Melancolia*. The composition draws on traditions of the funerary monument that had been revived by Roubiliac in his monument to General Hargrave in Westminster Abbey, completed about 1753. There are a number of iconographic parallels, but specially noteworthy is the witty parody of baroque sublimity by association: the tumbling sign-post of *The World's Tavern* has been substituted for the sculptor's crashing pyramid. The head of Father Time similarly burlesques *Fiammingo's Head*, which he had chosen for a key example of his linear theory. Among the scattered emblems of mortality is a legal commission declaring Nature bankrupt. Hogarth was always the observant realist, and the choice of Nature for his parting-shot against the connoisseurs, who employed their eyes and imagination only on art, was confirmed by the epitaph of Dr Johnson:

> The Hand of Art here torpid lies
> That traced the essential form of Grace;
> Here Death has closed the curious eyes
> That saw the manners in the face.

The editors wish to pay a special tribute to the monumental edition and commentary of Dr Ronald Paulson, and to his personal generosity to the present undertaking. His great edition supersedes the descriptions of the engravings in the British Museum *Catalogue of Political and Personal Satires* by Edward Hawkins and Frederick George Stephens (1873-83), a work which was unfortunately not illustrated. Dr Paulson has incorporated the findings of later scholars, and contributed many important ones of his own. His text is inevitably a long one, for it is the first to record all the major interpretations of successive generations of Hogarth commentators.

The concise commentary that is here offered to accompany the plates has required an editorial decision on many points. In some cases of interpretation no two commentators agree. The policy has been to choose the explanation or topical identification that seemed most reasonable, or the best supported; but no finality can be claimed.

The number of cases in which the editors have ventured to disagree with the attributions or dating of Dr Paulson are very few, and in each case he has stated fairly the evidence on both sides. The most important are *Taste, or Burlington Gate*, which has been reinstated in the *œuvre* of Hogarth, and the small illustrations to *Hudibras*, which the editors find difficult to believe were executed after the large plates. After the most careful collation of the text of Dr Paulson with that of earlier commentators, it is only fair to say that his learning is almost beyond praise in so immense an undertaking, which has required the full and detailed identification of separate states.

Hogarth made or authorized many changes in the subsequent states of his engravings, ranging from radical alterations or substitutions to technical and stylistic improvements. In order to give a representative indication of his method, different states of *The Rake's Progress* have been reproduced side by side, and in some other cases the original drawing has been reproduced for the same purpose. Where he does not make iconographic changes, his general tendency is to darken and heighten the chiaroscuro.

The measurements are given in inches and taken from the engraved surface of the picture area of the print unless the ornamental frame and its emblems are an essential part of the design, as in the *Industry and Idleness* prints. Unless otherwise stated, the medium is engraving on copper plate. The criteria for inclusion are, first, that the print was executed by Hogarth and, secondly, that it was published under his authority. Once he became famous and could afford to do so, he employed some of the finest engravers of his day to work from his paintings under his personal supervision. Because he supervised the engraving, and in some cases added personal touches, they cannot be wholly separated from his original work.

Many scholars and institutions have assisted in the preparation of this edition. Her Majesty the Queen has graciously permitted the editors to reproduce works in the royal collection, and Mr Wilmarth S. Lewis and the Marquess of Exeter have given their unfailing assistance to Hogarth students. A special debt is due to the Curator of Prints in the Lewis Walpole Library, Farmington, Connecticut, Mrs Richard D. Butterfield, for her scholarly assistance in answering queries. The major burden has fallen on the authorities of the Department of Prints in the British Museum. To this and other institutions named in the catalogue, notably the Victoria and Albert Museum, London, the Fitzwilliam Museum of Cambridge University, the New York Public Library, the Pierpont Morgan Library, the University of Iowa and the National Gallery of New South Wales, Sydney, a message of appreciation is gratefully extended.

Lastly, the editors are indebted to M. O'Meara for labours and an unfailing courtesy which have far exceeded those to be expected of a general editor, and to Mr P. Peyrelevade, who noted a number of inconsistencies and ambiguities in the original text.

The chief obligation is due to those scholars who have served the cause of Hogarth studies, headed by Dr Paulson. A select bibliography attempts to identify the most important of these studies, especially those which contain fuller bibliographies of sources and commentaries.

JOSEPH BURKE

SELECT BIBLIOGRAPHY

RONALD PAULSON. *Hogarth's Graphic Works*. 2 vols. New Haven and London: Yale University Press, 1965.

E. HAWKINS and F.G. STEPHENS. *Catalogue of Prints and Drawings in the British Museum. Division I. Political and Personal Satires*. Printed by order of the Trustees, London, vols. II to IV, 1873–83.
This contains the most detailed description of the major satires, but does not embrace the whole field of Hogarth studies as does the comprehensive Paulson edition.

FREDERICK ANTAL. *Hogarth and his Place in European Art*. London: Routledge and Kegan Paul. 1962.

R.B. BECKETT. *Hogarth*. London: Routledge and Kegan Paul. 1949.
This is confined to the paintings but reproduces all those from which the engravings were made, except *The Harlot's Progress*, which was destroyed by fire at Fonthill in 1755.

A.P. OPPÉ. *The Drawings of William Hogarth*. London: Phaidon Press, 1948.
This reproduces a large number of the original drawings from which the prints were made.

JOSEPH BURKE. *The Analysis of Beauty, with the Rejected Passages from the Manuscript Drafts and Autobiographical Notes*. Oxford: at the Clarendon Press, 1955.

HILDE KURZ. 'Italian Models of Hogarth's Picture Stories' in *Journal of the Warburg and Courtauld Institutes*, 1952.

F. ANTAL. 'The Moral Purpose of Hogarth's Art' in *Journal of the Warburg and Courtauld Institutes*, 1952.

E. WIND. 'Borrowed Attitudes in Hogarth and Reynolds' in *Journal of the Warburg and Courtauld Institutes*, 1938–39.

JOSEPH BURKE, 'Hogarth' in *Enciclopedia Universale dell'Arte*, vol. VII, Istituto per la Collaborazione Culturale, Venezia–Roma, and in *Encyclopedia of World Art*, vol. VII, McGraw-Hill Book Co. Inc.; New York, Toronto, London, 1958.
This has some bibliographical reference to Hogarth's Continental critics and commentators, notably G.C. LICHTENBERG, *Ausführliche Erklärung der hogarthischen Kupferstiche*, Göttingen, 1794–1833, translated into English with a notable introduction by INNES and GUSTAV HERDAN, *Lichtenberg's Commentaries on Hogarth's Engravings*, London: the Cresset Press, 1966. In France this commentary became better known than HENRI JANSEN, *Analyse de la beauté*, 2 vols., Paris, 1806, the second volume of which contains the commentary on the prints compiled by the learned librarian of Talleyrand.

Ellis Gamble
GOLDSMITH,
at the Golden Angel in
Cranbourn-Street,
LEICESTER-FIELDS.
Makes, Buys & Sells all
sorts of Plate, Rings, &
Jewells, &c.

Ellis Gamble
ORFÈURE,
a L'Enseigne de l'Ange d'Or
dans Cranbourn-Street,
LEICESTER-FIELDS.
Fait, Achete, & Vend toutes
sortes d'Argenterie, Bagues
& Bijouxs, &c.

2

3

4

5

6

7

8

George Lambart

9

10

12

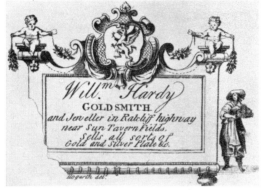

11

13

14

15

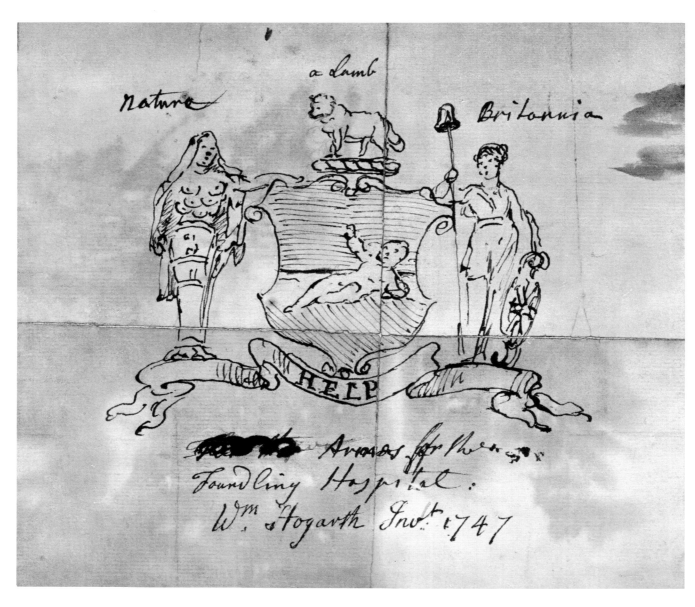

15*

16

16 detail

17

18

19

20

21

22

22a

22b

22c

22d

23

25*

25

25 detail

26

26a

26b

26c

26d

26e

28

30

30 detail

32

32 detail

34

34 detail

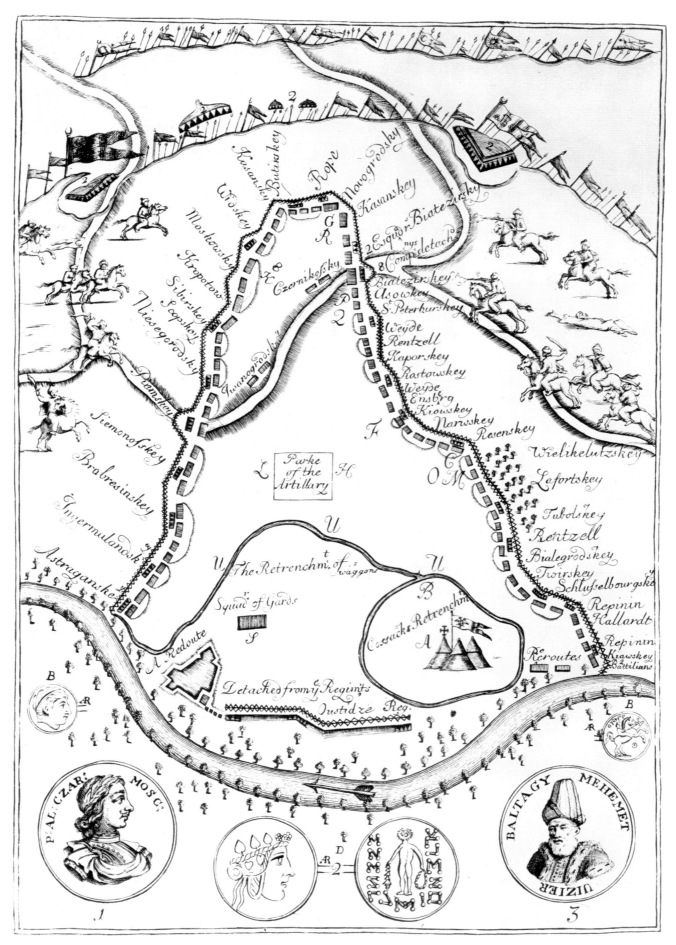

Kasanskey
Butirskey
Rofe
Novogrodsky
Wlofkey
Kasanskey
Mloskowskey
2 Esqudr Biatezirsky
nys Compedetach
Krypotow
Czernikofsky
Biatezirskey
Silirskey
Asowkey
Scopskoy
St Peterburskey
Niesegrodskey
Weyde
Rentzell
Kaporskey
Rastowskey
Iwanogrodskh
Weyse
Ensbrg
Kiowskey
Plawskou
Narwskey
Resenskey
Siemonofskey
Wielikelutzskey
Brabresinskey
Lafortskey
Ingermulanosk
Tubolskey
Rentzell
Astraganskey
Bialegrodskey
Twirskey
Schlufselbourgske
Repinin
Hallardt
Repinin
Kiowskey
2 Battilians

G R
P
2
F
O M
B

L Parke of the Artillary H

U
U The Retrenchm.t of waggons
Squadr of Gards S
A Redoute
U
B Cossacks Retrenchm A
Redoutes
Detached from y.e Regim.ts
Iustid z.e Reg.

Ps AL: CZAR: MOSC:

D
AR
2

BALTAGY MEHEMET VIZIER

1
3

35

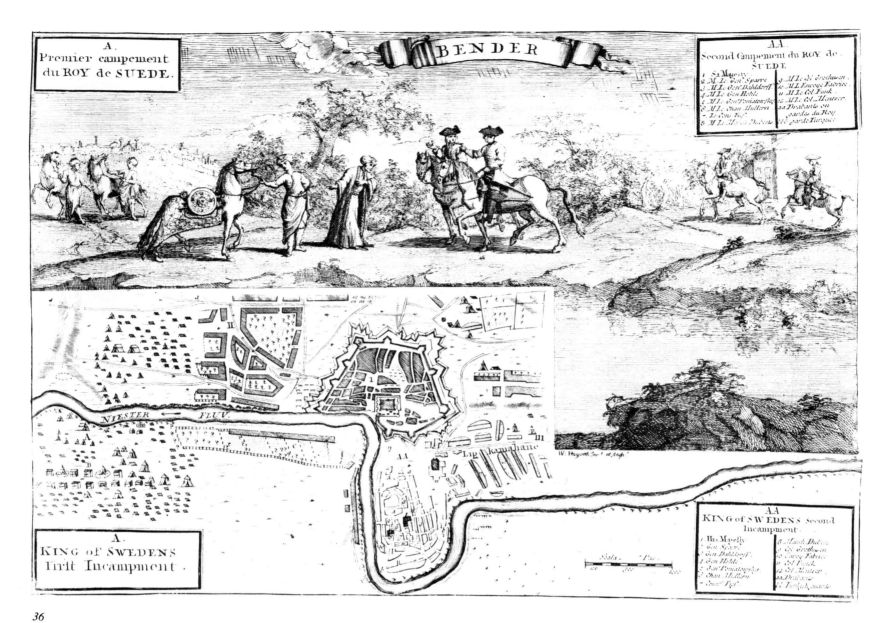

BENDER

36

36 detail

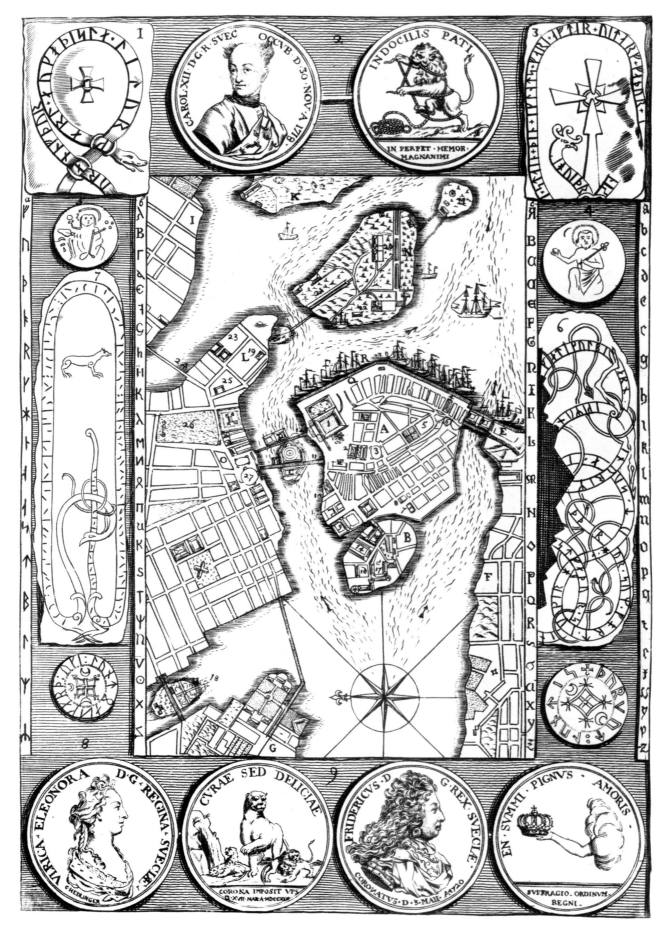

1

2 CAROL·XII·D·G·R·SVEC OCCVB·D·30·NOV·A·1718 INDOCILIS PATI IN PERPET·MEMOR MAGNANIMI

3

4

7

8

9 VLRICA·ELEONORA D·G·REGINA·SVECLÆ CVRÆ SED DELICIÆ CORONA IMPOSIT VPS D·XVII·MAR·A·MDCCXIX FRIDERICVS·D·G·REX·SVECLÆ CORONATVS·D·3·MAII·A·1720 EN·SVMMI·PIGNVS·AMORIS SVFRAGIO·ORDINVM REGNI

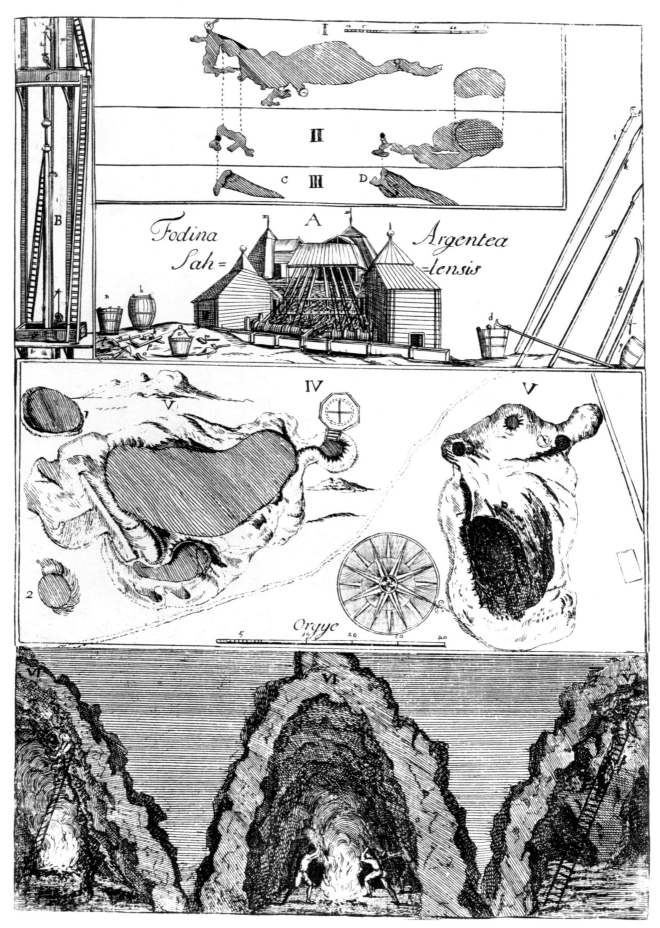

Fodina Sah=lensis

Argentea =lensis

Oryge

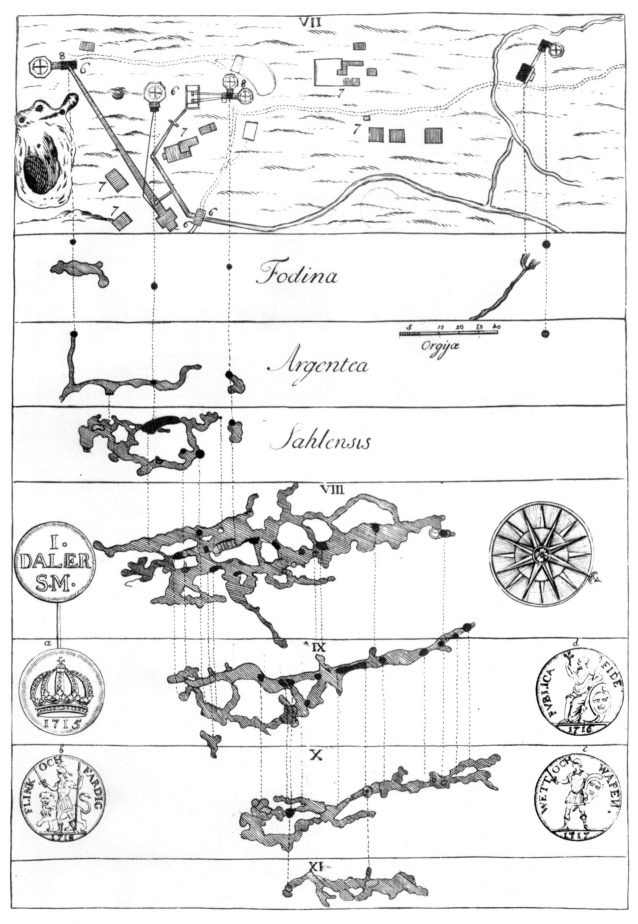

VII

Fodina

Argentea

Sahlensis

Orgijæ

VIII

I.
DALER
S·M·

IX

1715

PVBLICA FIDE
1716

FLINK OCH FARDIG

X

WETT OCH WAPEN

XI

39

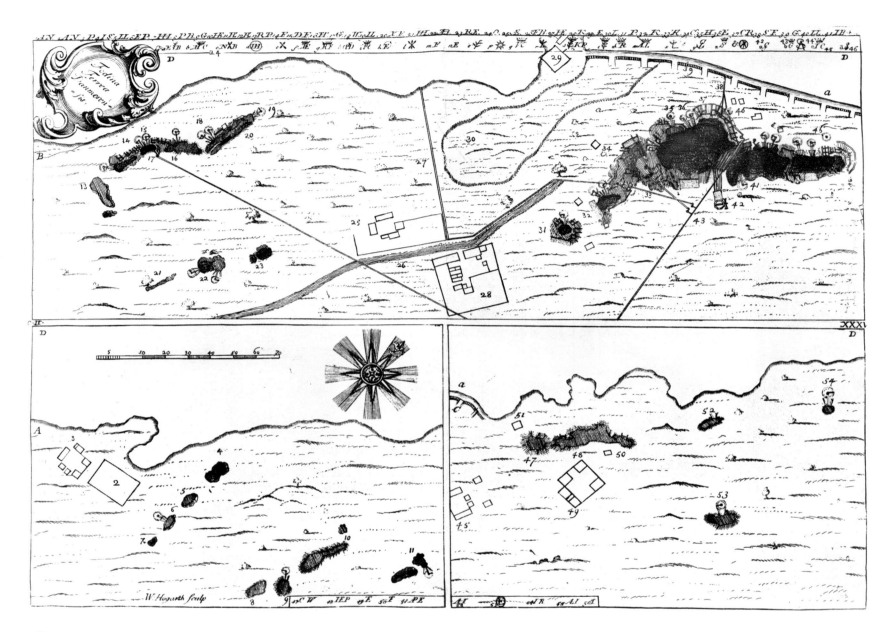

W. Hogarth sculp

40

41

41 detail

42

43

45

44

46

47

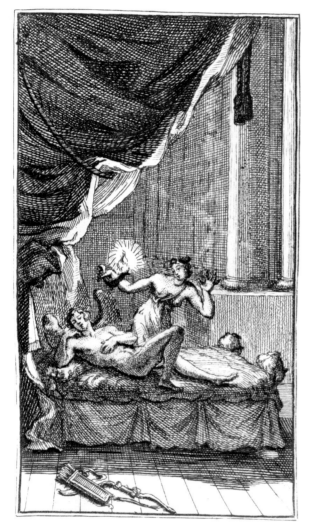

48

49

ST MATTHEW Ch. 21. Verſe 28.
Son, go Work to day in
my Vineyard.

50

52

54

55

56

57

58

60

61

62

63

64

65

66

67

68

69

70

71

72

73   74   75

76   77

78

79

81

80

82

83

84

85

86

87

88

89

90

91

92

93

95

94

96

97*

97

97 detail

98

98 *detail*

100

100 detail

102

102 detail

104

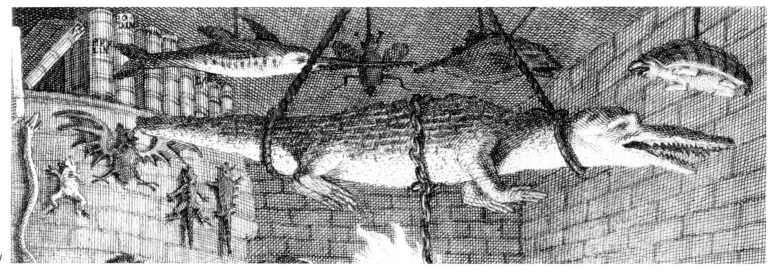

104
detail

106

106 detail

108

108 detail

110 detail

110

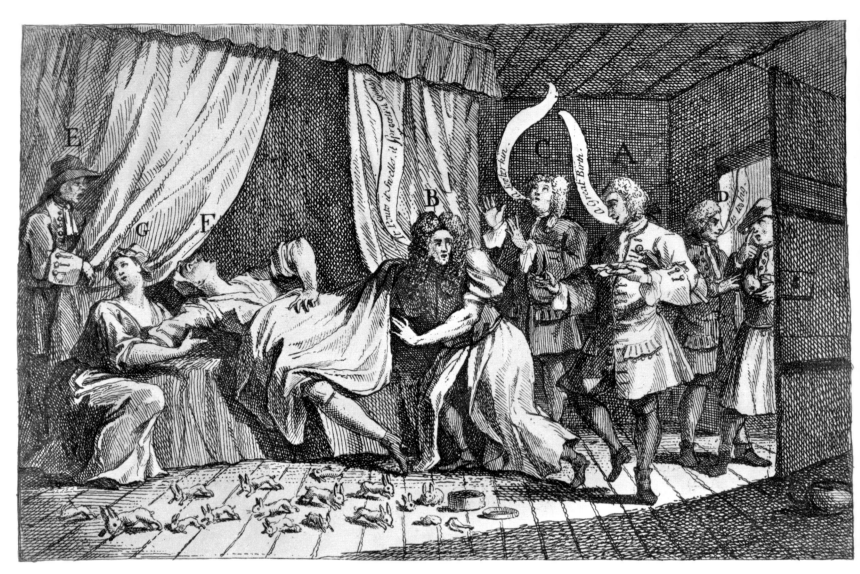

112

112 detail

114

114 detail

115

Musick
Introduc'd
to Apollo
by
Minerva
1727.

Hogarth Fec

116

117

ΗΣΙΟΔΟΣ

Ex musæo Pembrokiano   W. Hogarth Sculp.

118

119

121

122

123

123 detail

124

124 detail

125

126

127

128

129

130

130*

131

132

132 detail

133

133 detail

134

134 detail

135

135 detail

136

136 detail

137

137 detail

138

138 detail

139

139 detail

141

141 detail

142

143

144

145

146

147

147 detail

148

148 detail

149

149 detail

150

150 detail

151

151 detail

152

152 detail

153

153 detail

154

154 detail

155

155 detail

156

156 detail

157

157 detail

158

158 detail

159

159 detail

160

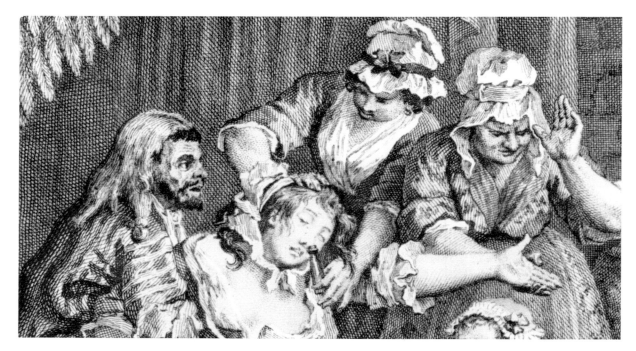

160 detail

161

161 detail

162

162 detail

165 *detail*

166 *detail*

167

ET PLURIMA MORTIS IMAGO

169

169 detail

170

171

172

W. Hogarth Inven.ᵗ et Sculp.ᵗ

173

174

175

177

177 detail

178 detail

179 detail

180 detail

181

181 detail

183

184

184 detail

1 2 3

A Scale of feet

185

186

187

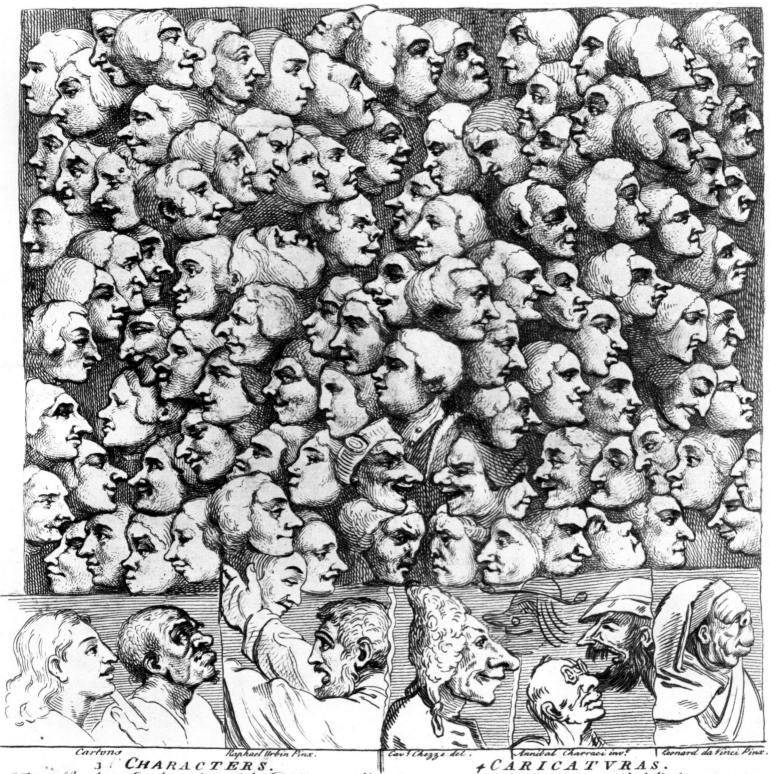

Cartons   Raphael Urbin Pinx.   Cav.ͤ Chezze del.   Annibal Charraci inv.ͭ   Leonard da Vinci Pinx.

3 CHARACTERS.   4 CARICATVRAS.

For a farthar Explanation of the Difference Betwixt Character & Caricatura See y.ͤ Preface to Jo.ͤ Andrews.

W.ͫ Hogarth Fecit 1743

Rec.ᵈ April 12 1743 of John Huggins Esq.ˢ

Half a Guinea being the first Payment for Six Prints Called MARRIAGE

A LA MODE which I Promise to deliver when finish'd on Receiving half a Guinea more.

N.B. The price will be one Guinea and an half after the time of Subscribing.

W.ͫ Hogarth

189

189 detail

The Battle of the Pictures

190

The Bearer hereof is Intitled to
a Print twenty Inches by 15 and an half, of Mr. Garrick,
in the Character of Richard the Third, Engraved after a
Picture Painted By Mr. Hogarth

7-6

191

192

193*

193

193 detail

194*

194

194 detail

195*

195

195 detail

196*

196

196 detail

197*

197

197 detail

198*

198

199

199 detail

202

202 detail

203*

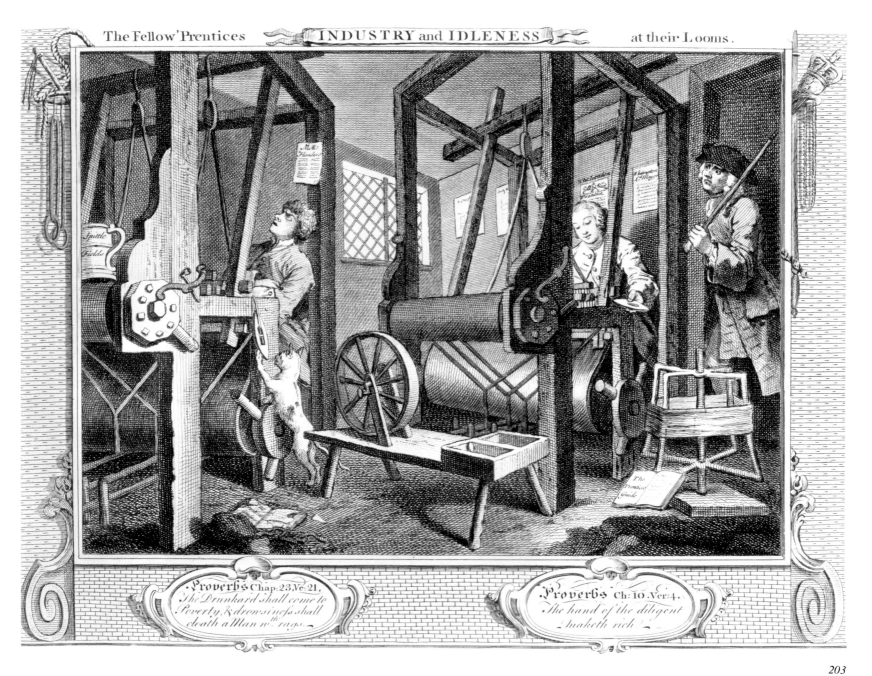

Proverbs Chap: 23.Ver: 21.
The Drunkard shall come to
Poverty, & drowsiness shall
cloath a Man w.th rags.

Proverbs Ch: 10 .Ver: 4.
The hand of the diligent
maketh rich.

203

203 detail

Pſalm cxix Ver: 97.
O How I love thy Law it is my
meditation all the day.

Proverbs Ch: XIX. Ve: 29.
Judgments are prepar'd for Scorners
& Stripes for the back of Fools.

205

205 detail

Matthew CHAP: XXV. Ve: 21.
Well done thou good and faithfull
Servant thou hast been faithfull
over a few things, I will make thee
Ruler over many things.

206

206 detail

The IDLE 'PRENTICE turn'd away, and sent to Sea.

Proverbs Chap: X. Ve: 1.
A Foolish Son is the heaviness
of his Mother.

208*

The INDUSTRIOUS 'PRENTICE out of his Time, & Married to his Master's Daughter.

Goodchild & West

Proverbs CH:XII. Ver: 4.
The Virtuous Woman is a Crown to her Husband.

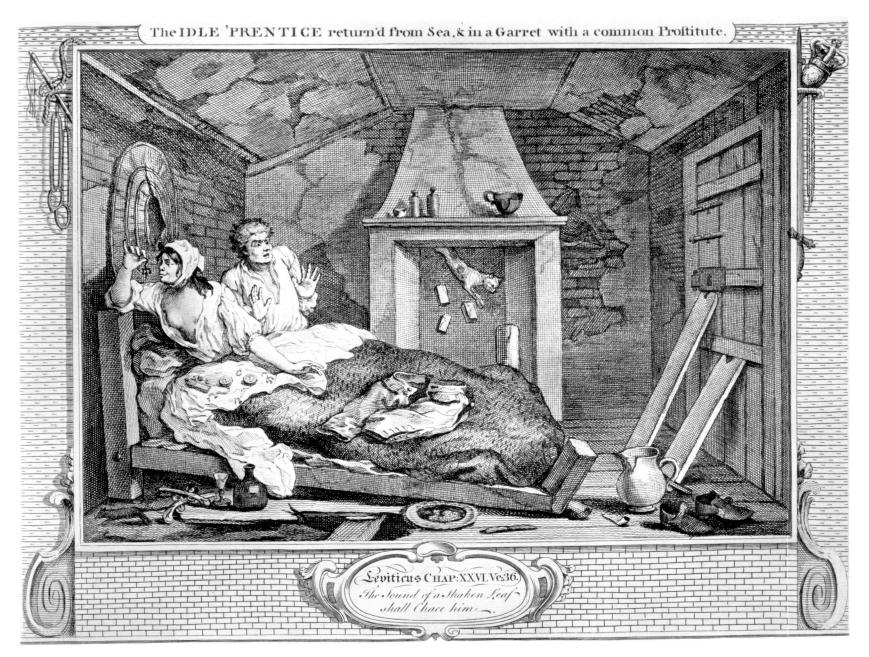

Leviticus CHAP: XXVI. Ve: 36.
The Sound of a Shaken Leaf
shall Chace him.

209

209 detail

The INDUSTRIOUS 'PRENTICE grown rich, & Sheriff of London.

Proverbs Ch:IV.Ver:7,8.
With all thy getting get understanding.
Exalt her, & she shall promote thee: she
shall bring thee to honour when
thou dost Embrace her.

210

210 detail

The IDLE 'PRENTICE betray'd by his Whore, & taken in a Night Cellar with his Accomplice.

Proverbs CHAP: VI. Ve: 26.
The Adulteress will hunt for
the precious life.

211

211 detail

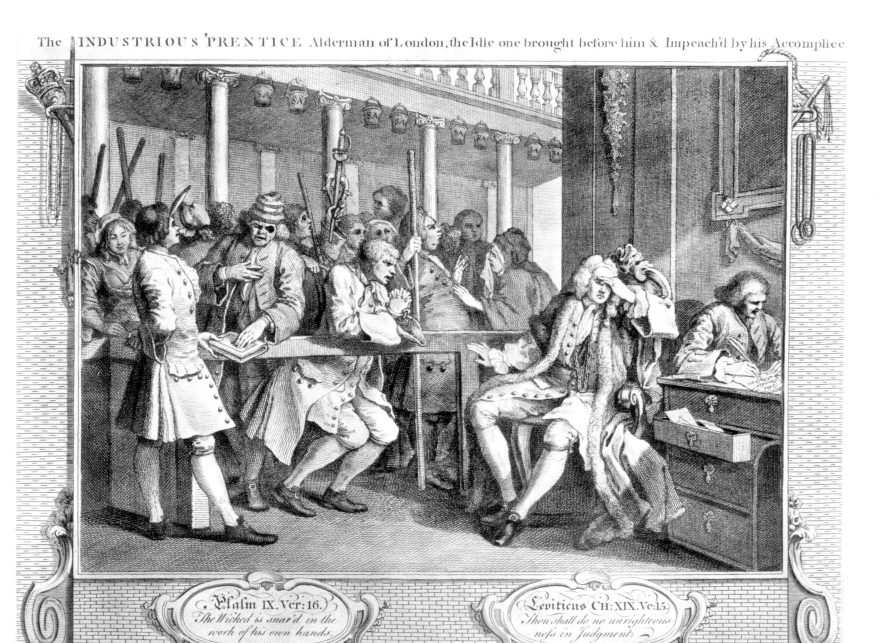

Psalm IX. Ver: 16.
The Wicked is snar'd in the
work of his own hands.

Leviticus CH: XIX. Ve: 15.
Thou shalt do no unrighteousness in Judgment.

212

212 detail

The IDLE 'PRENTICE Executed at Tyburn.

Proverbs Chap: I. Vers: 27,28.
When fear cometh as desolation, and their
destruction cometh as a Whirlwind; when
distress cometh upon them, then they shall
call upon God, but he will not answer.

213

213 detail

The INDUSTRIOUS 'PRENTICE Lord-Mayor of London.

Proverbs CHAP: III. Ver: 16.
Length of days is in her right hand, and
in her left hand Riches and Honour.

214

214 detail

JACOBUS GIBBS
ARCHITECTUS.
17 47

217

217 detail

218 detail

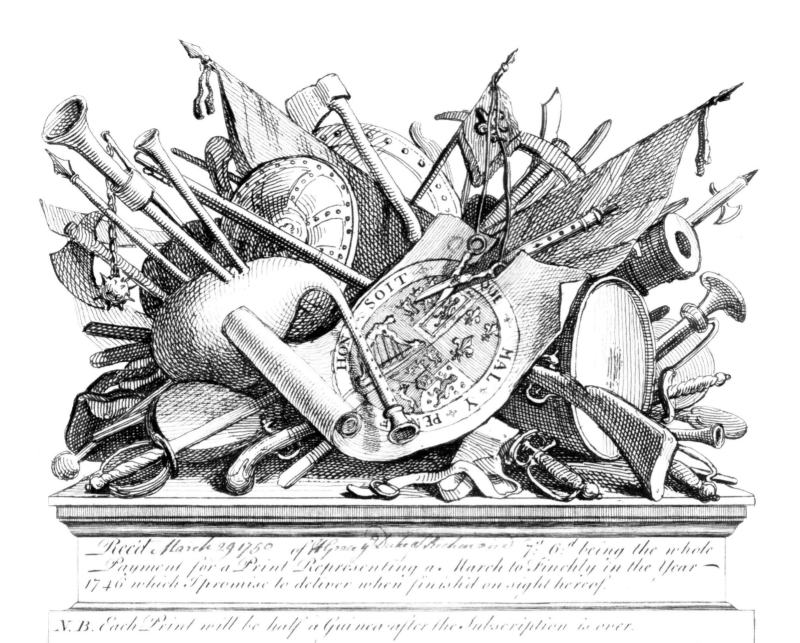

Rec'd March 29 1750 of _His Grace y.e Duke of Richmond_ 7.s 6.d _being the whole_
Payment for a Print Representing a March to Finchley in the Year —
1746 _which I promise to deliver when finish'd on sight hereof._

N.B. _Each Print will be half a Guinea after the Subscription is over._

219

220

221 detail

223

223 detail

224 *

225

224 *detail*

225 detail

226 detail

227 detail

228

228 detail

229

229 detail

231

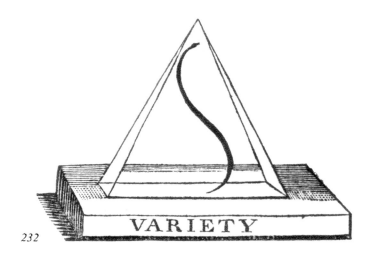

232

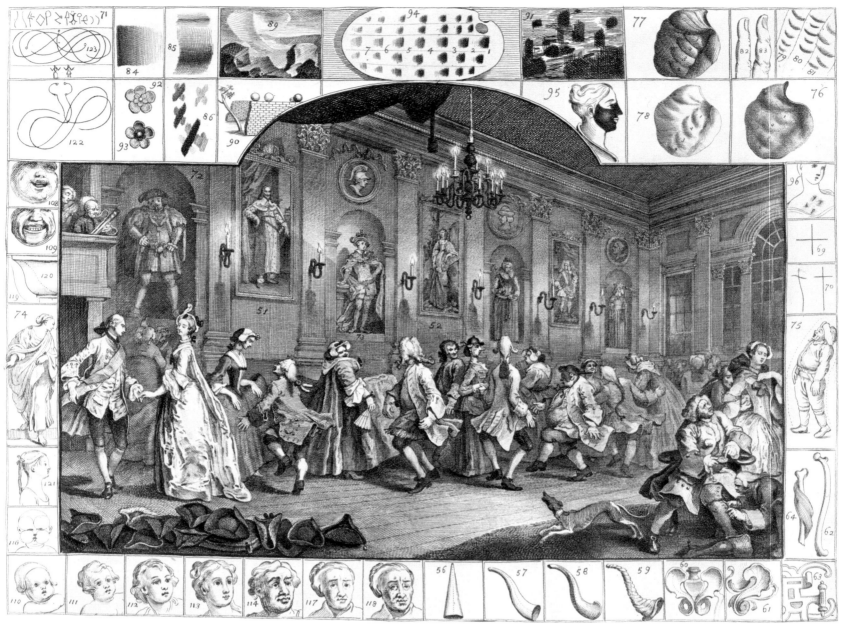

234

234 detail

Design'd, Etch'd & Publish'd, as the Act directs, by W.ᵐ Hogarth, March 20.ᵗʰ 1754.

In humble & grateful Acknowledgment of the Grace & Goodness of the *Legislature*, Manifested, In the *Act of Parliament* for the Encouragement of the Arts of Designing Engraving &c; Obtain'd by the Endeavours & almost at the Sole Expence of the designer of this Print in the Year 1735: By which not only the Professors of those Arts were rescued from the Tyranny Frauds & Piracies	of Monopolising Dealers and Legally entitled to the Fruits of their own Labours, but Genius & Industry were also prompted by ỹ most noble & generous Inducements to exert themselves, Emulation was Excited, Ornamental Compositions were better understood, and every Manufacture where Fancy has any concern was gradually raisd to a pitch of perfection before unknown, Insomuch that those of *Great Britain* are at present the most Elegant and the most in Esteem of any in *Europe*.

Rec.ᵈ 3ᵈ May 1754 of M.ʳ W.ᵐ Dale 5ˢ being the first Payment for a Print representing an Election Entertainment, which I Promise to deliver when finish'd on the receipt of Five Shillings & Six Pence more.

236

238

238 detail

239

240

240 detail

241

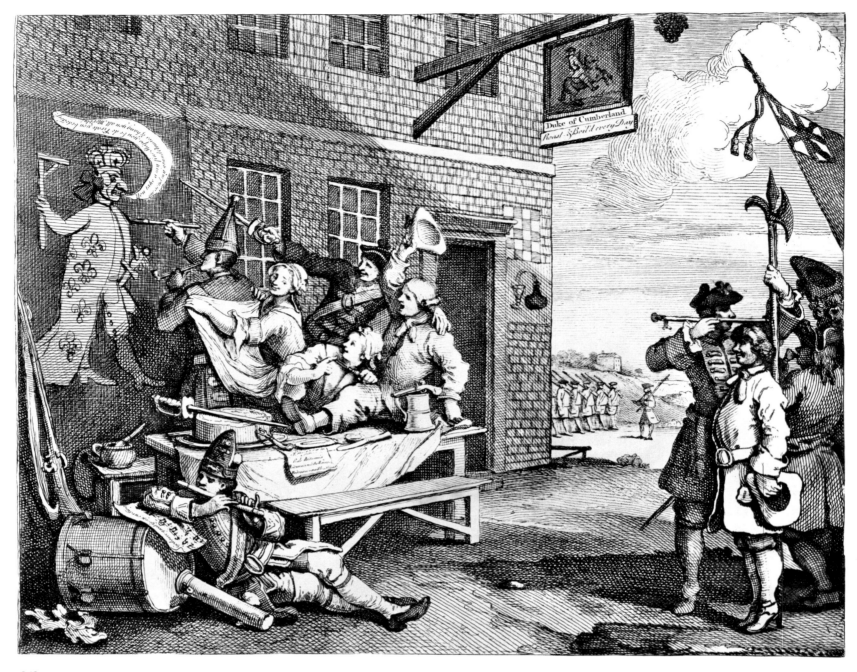

242

242 detail

243

243 detail

244

245

246

246 detail

247

247*

248

249

249 detail

As Statues moulder into Worth. *P:W.*

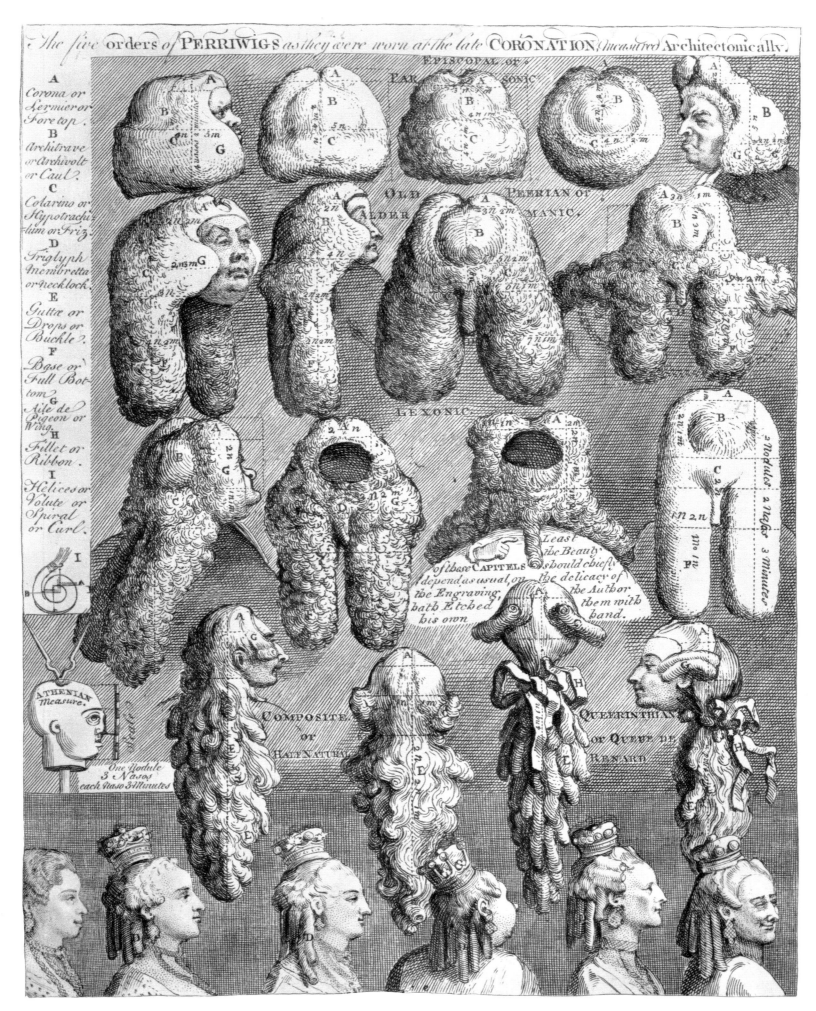

251

252

253

252 detail

253 detail

254

255

256

256 detail

257

257 detail

258

258 detail

259

259 detail

260

261

262

Great George Street. A List of the
Subscribers to the North Britons.

A New way to Pay old Debts, a
Comedy, by Maßenger.

AN
EPISTLE
TO
HOGARTH
BY
C.CHURCHILL

Lye
I

Lye
3

Lye
5

Lye
8

FALSE

Lye
IO

Lye
12

LYE
15

Lye

264

264 *detail*

265

266

267

267 detail

NOTES ON THE PLATES

NOTES ON THE PLATES

* denotes a painting, drawing or sketch

1. SHOPCARD FOR ELLIS GAMBLE. *c.* 1723. Attributed to Hogarth. $7\frac{3}{8} \times 5\frac{7}{8}$ ins. British Museum.

2. ARMS OF GAMBLE. Attributed to Hogarth. Date unknown. $2\frac{1}{2} \times 2\frac{1}{8}$ ins. British Museum.

3. ARMS OF TATTON. Date unknown. $2\frac{3}{8}$ ins. diam. British Museum.
   The two slaves derive from Jacques Callot's title-page for the *Statutes of the Order of the Knights of St Stephen* (Paulson 1).

4. WILLIAM HOGARTH'S SHOPCARD. April 1720. $3 \times 3\frac{15}{16}$ ins. British Museum.

5. SHOPCARD FOR JAMES BARTLETT, DRUGGIST. 1720. $3 \times 3\frac{3}{4}$ ins. British Museum. Attributed to Hogarth. Compare the angel in Ellis Gamble's shopcard (No. 1).

6. ARMS OF THE DUCHESS OF KENDALL. After 1723. $4\frac{3}{4} \times 5\frac{3}{8}$ ins. British Museum.
   Countess Ehrengard Melusina von der Schulenberg was created Duchess of Kendall in 1719 and Princess of Eberstein in January 1723, the coronet and lion rampant denoting her royal rank in the German peerage. The tall thin mistress of George I, she was nicknamed the Maypole.

7. IMPRESSION FROM A TANKARD BELONGING TO THE CLARE MARKET ACTORS' CLUB. Date unknown. $4\frac{1}{4} \times 6\frac{1}{2}$ ins. Royal Library, Windsor Castle.
   In the oval, Laban and his sheep (*Genesis*, 29: 13–14); Painting on the left, Sculpture on the right.
   Clare Market was a butchers' market, hence Laban and his sheep. Between Drury Lane and Lincoln's Inn Fields Theatres, it was famous for its actors' club, joined by authors and artists. Hogarth, always keenly interested in the stage, is said to have frequented the tavern meetings while he was still an apprentice.

8. ARMS OF COUNT LIPPE-SCHAUENBERG. After January 1723. Attributed to Hogarth. $2\frac{1}{8} \times 3$ ins. British Museum.
   The arms of the son-in-law and daughter of the Duchess of Kendall, to whose ennoblement as a Princess of the Germanic Empire the lion rampant in the shield in the centre of the wife's arms refers.

9. BOOKPLATE FOR GEORGE LAMBERT. *c.* 1725. Etching. $2\frac{13}{16} \times 2\frac{3}{4}$ ins. Royal Library, Windsor Castle.
   George Lambert was a landscape painter closely associated with Hogarth, who compared him with Claude and shared his devotion to the theatre. The supporters are Music and Painting.

10. PAULET BOOKPLATE. Date unknown. Etching. $2\frac{1}{8} \times 2\frac{3}{8}$ ins. British Museum.
    Possibly for Charles Paulet, who became third Duke of Bolton in 1722 and appears in Hogarth's *Beggar's Opera*.

11. SHOPCARD FOR WILLIAM HARDY, GOLDSMITH. Date unknown. $2 \times 2\frac{5}{8}$ ins. Royal Library, Windsor Castle.

12. SHOPCARD FOR THE ARTIST'S SISTERS, MARY AND ANN HOGARTH. *c.* 1730. Etching. $3\frac{5}{8} \times 4\frac{1}{8}$ ins. British Museum.

13. SHOPCARD FOR MRS HOLT'S ITALIAN WAREHOUSE. Date unknown. $3\frac{3}{4} \times 5$ ins. W. S. Lewis collection.
    Florence entrusts her orders to Mercury, whose figure is taken from Perino del Vaga's cycle *The Loves of the Gods*, engraved by Caraglio.

14. ARMS OF JOHN HOLLAND, HERALD PAINTER. Date unknown. $4\frac{5}{8} \times 4\frac{1}{8}$ ins. British Museum.

15. ARMS OF THE FOUNDLING HOSPITAL. By an unknown engraver after a drawing by Hogarth. 1747. $4\frac{5}{8} \times 8\frac{1}{2}$ ins. W. S. Lewis collection.

15.*ARMS OF THE FOUNDLING HOSPITAL. Pen sketch for the above. Signed and dated 1747. $6\frac{1}{4} \times 7$ ins. The Marquess of Exeter.
    The sketch and engraving have been included for comparison among the early works, although much later. Hogarth was a Foundation Governor of the Hospital and in its favour made an exception to his rule not to design coats of arms after he had become famous as a painter.

16. THE GREAT SEAL OF ENGLAND, 1728/9. Impression from silver plate engraving. Second state. $9\frac{1}{4}$ ins. diam. British Museum.

Whenever the Great Seal was redesigned after the death of a king, the Chancellor of the Exchequer was allowed to convert the old matrix into plate as a memorial of his office. Sir Robert Walpole exercised this right on receiving the new Seal on 15 August 1728, and employed Hogarth to design the centrepiece enclosing the two sides of the Seal. The Walpole Salver, which is considerably larger than the centrepiece, is now in the Victoria and Albert Museum.

17. A SCENE FROM 'THE RAPE OF THE LOCK' BY ALEXANDER POPE. Engraving for the lid of a snuff box, illustrating Canto IV, line 121 *et seq.* Date unknown. $2\frac{1}{4} \times 3\frac{1}{8}$ ins. British Museum.
This is possibly the earliest of Hogarth's illustrations of a literary text, and was acquired by Horace Walpole, who listed it as one of his first works of the kind.

18. SEARCH NIGHT. Attributed to Hogarth. Engraving for the lid of a snuff box. Date unknown. $2\frac{5}{8} \times 3\frac{7}{8}$ ins. British Museum.
The watch arrests a couple who have been surprised *in flagrante delicto*.

19. BENEFIT TICKET FOR THE COMIC ACTOR JAMES SPILLER. Possibly March 1720. Etching, second state. $3\frac{3}{8} \times 4\frac{3}{8}$ ins. British Museum.
The financially embarrassed actor, whom Hogarth knew as a member of the Clare Market Actors' Club, stands under Fortune's wheel and balance selling tickets. One side of the balance is heavily weighed down with bills for gin, tobacco and fine clothes. The flambeau will be used to ignite the gunpowder on the ground if the tickets are left unsold.

20. SHOPCARD FOR RICHARD LEE, TOBACCONIST. Attributed to Hogarth. Date unknown. $3\frac{1}{4} \times 3\frac{7}{8}$ ins. British Museum.

21. MOCK INVITATION TO A FUNERAL. Attributed to Hogarth. Date unknown. Etched and engraved. $4\frac{5}{8} \times 6\frac{1}{2}$ ins. British Museum.
All the early commentators say that this is undoubtedly by Hogarth, but the style is unusual. It may be a *jeu d'esprit* in collaboration.

22. THE FOUR ELEMENTS. Date unknown. Juno ($2\frac{3}{16} \times 1\frac{15}{16}$ ins.), Neptune ($2\frac{1}{16} \times 1\frac{7}{8}$ ins.), Tellus ($3\frac{3}{4} \times 6\frac{7}{8}$ ins.), and Vulcan ($4\frac{1}{4} \times 4\frac{3}{4}$ ins.), around Jacob and Laban's flock. W. S. Lewis collection.
Probably a collector's arrangement of impressions from a silver platter round the inset for the Arms of the Clare Market Actors' Club (see No. 7).

23. AN ALLEGORY OF GEORGE, PRINCE OF WALES AS THE FUTURE PROTECTOR OF THE REALM. Before 1727. Signed. $5\frac{3}{4} \times 7$ ins. British Museum.
The portrait of George by Sir Godfrey Kneller is attended by Hercules surmounting the Hydra of War; Britannia; Peace raising an olive branch and lowering a torch; and the Three Graces with emblems of Trade, the Arts and Monarchy.

24. THE SOUTH SEA SCHEME. 1721. Etching and engraving. First state. Signed. $8\frac{1}{2} \times 12\frac{1}{8}$ ins. British Museum.
A satire, probably commissioned by a printseller, on the collapse of the South Sea Company or 'Bubble' in August 1720, a speculative undertaking based on the Scotsman John Law's Company of the West, or Mississippi Company, founded in France.
A wheel of fortune is used as a merry-go-round turned by directors of the South Sea Company. The passengers are subscribers and include a prostitute, a clergyman, a shoeblack and a Scots nobleman with his blue garter. To the left, a devil cuts off pieces from Fortune's body and casts them to the crowd below. In the centre, Honesty is broken on the wheel, and to the right, Honour is being flogged. St Paul's Cathedral is in the distance, the Guildhall and Monument to left and right. The numerous episodes have the common theme of gambling and swindling.

25.*THE LOTTERY. 1721. Drawing in reverse for the engraving. Pen, grey wash, corrections with brown ink and red chalk. $9 \times 12\frac{3}{4}$ ins. The Royal Library, Windsor Castle.

25. THE LOTTERY. 1721. Signed. Second state. $8\frac{13}{16} \times 12\frac{5}{8}$ ins. British Museum.
State lotteries were used to raise funds for national purposes between 1694 and 1826, and the drawing of prizes took place in the Guildhall. Wantonness with a windmill in her hand draws a number from the first wheel, blindfolded Fortune draws a ticket marked either blank or prize from the second. Upon the pedestal National Credit is supported by Justice and Apollo, who points out an allegorical picture to Britannia. Below, Suspense is turned on a turnstile by Fear and Hope alternately.
The print parodies Raphael's School of Athens and *Disputà*, and is the first of a series of Old Master parodies that Hogarth was to continue throughout his life.

26. SIX ILLUSTRATIONS FOR THE SECOND EDITION OF DR WILLIAM KING'S 'PANTHEON'. Before 1722. Etching. Nos. 1–3, $4\frac{5}{8} \times 2\frac{5}{8}$ ins.; No. 4, $4\frac{5}{8} \times 2\frac{3}{4}$ ins.; Nos. 5 and 6, $4\frac{3}{4} \times 2\frac{3}{4}$ ins. British Museum.
William King was a satirist in the manner of Jonathan Swift.

27–41. FIFTEEN ILLUSTRATIONS FOR THE 'TRAVELS THROUGH EUROPE, ASIA AND INTO PART OF AFRICA', BY AUBREY DE LA MOTRAYE, 2 VOLS. 1723/4. From a copy in the British Museum.
Since the publication of his edition, Dr Paulson has discovered an announcement in the *Post Boy* for 31 July–3 August 1714, advertising the publication of a second edition with cuts 'engraved by a French-Man lately arrived from Paris'. No copy of this edition has as yet been traced. Until a comparison can be made with the plates in the third edition attributed by all commentators to Hogarth, some doubt on the attribution to his hand must arise.
De la Motraye's *Travels*, published both in English and French, was a Grand Tour guide book with an emphasis on costume, history, resources, manners and exotic *mirabilia*, copiously illustrated by several artists. Hogarth's illustrations are clearly influenced by Bernard Picart's *Cérémonies et coûtumes religieuses*, Amsterdam, 1723.

27. AN EMERALD VESSEL. Engraved by J. Grisoni, after Hogarth's design. $4\frac{13}{16} \times 15\frac{1}{2}$ ins.
The original in Genoa Cathedral was said to be a present from the Queen of Sheba to Solomon, and to have been used by Christ in the Last Supper.

28. A GREEK PATRIARCHAL CROWN. First state. Signed. $13\frac{3}{8} \times 10\frac{13}{16}$ ins.

29. A TURKISH BATH. First state. $9\frac{7}{8} \times 6\frac{13}{16}$ ins.

30. A NATIVE DANCE. First state. Signed. $9\frac{3}{4} \times 13\frac{5}{8}$ ins.
The dancers are Turks and Greeks in Smyrna.

31. A PROCESSION THROUGH THE HIPPODROME, CONSTANTINOPLE. First state. Signed. $9\frac{3}{4} \times 13\frac{1}{4}$ ins.

32. THE INSIDE OF A TURKISH MOSQUE. First state. $9\frac{7}{8} \times 13\frac{7}{8}$ ins.

33. THE CROWNING OF THE SULTAN ACHMET IN THE MOSQUE OF YUP. Called 'Figures in Turbans'. First state. Signed. $9\frac{5}{8} \times 6\frac{7}{8}$ ins.

34. THE SERAGLIO. First state. Signed. $9\frac{3}{4} \times 13\frac{1}{2}$ ins.
Hogarth has shown a male face peeping through a window.

35. PARKE OF THE ARTILLERY. First state. Signed. $9\frac{13}{16} \times 6\frac{7}{8}$ ins.
Plan of the battle between Peter the Great of Russia and the Vizier Mehemet Baltadji, brought about by Charles XII of Sweden.

36. CHARLES XII AT BENDER. Signed. $9\frac{3}{4} \times 13\frac{9}{16}$ ins.

37. MAP OF STOCKHOLM. First state. Signed. $9\frac{11}{16} \times 6\frac{3}{4}$ ins.
Some of the coins and ornaments show runic characters.

38. A SILVER MINE AT SALA – I. First state. Signed. $9\frac{11}{16} \times 6\frac{13}{16}$ ins.

39. A SILVER MINE AT SALA – II. First state. Signed. $9\frac{11}{16} \times 6\frac{1}{2}$ ins.

40. A DANISH IRON MINE. First state. Signed. $9\frac{15}{16} \times 13\frac{5}{8}$ ins.

41. A LAPLAND HUT. First state. Signed. $9\frac{7}{8} \times 13\frac{1}{2}$ ins.

42. MASQUERADES AND OPERAS, OR THE TASTE OF THE TOWN. February 1723/4. Etching and engraving. First state. Signed. $5 \times 6\frac{11}{16}$ ins. British Museum.
According to Hogarth, this was 'the first plate I published', i.e., on his own account, not as a commission.
Two crowds assemble in front of Burlington Gate, the entrance to the mansion of the Earl of Burlington in Piccadilly. On the pediment of the gate Raphael and Michelangelo direct admiring gazes at William Kent, who was the favourite painter of Burlington.
One crowd is seeking admittance to a conjuring display by Fawkes, whose name is wittily misspelled 'Faux', and to a masquerade organized by the Swiss impresario Heidegger; the other is crowding into a pantomime, *Harlequin Dr*

Faustus. A woman pushes a wheelbarrow containing 'Waste Paper for Shops'; it is filled with the works of Shakespeare, Dryden, Otway, Congreve and Ben Jonson (Pasquin in the first state).

On the signboard in front of the entrance to the Masquerade, the Earl of Peterborough and two other noblemen are on their knees and offer £8,000 to the Italian soprano Francesca Cuzzoni.

The moral is that aristocratic patrons are infatuated with foreign modes and neglect native talent.

43–9. SEVEN ILLUSTRATIONS FOR CHARLES GILDON'S 'NEW METAMORPHOSIS', 1724. March 1723/4. Etching and engraving. British Museum. The book was a rococo parody on *The Golden Ass* of Apuleius. All are signed except No. 46.

43. FRONTISPIECE. A copy of the frontispiece of the 1708 edition, with the addition of a church. $5\frac{3}{8} \times 3$ ins.

44. CORRUPT PRIESTS AND GALLANTS CELEBRATE THE FEAST OF ST THERESA IN AN ITALIAN CHURCH. $5\frac{3}{8} \times 3$ ins.

45. BANDITS ABDUCTING CAMILLA. $5\frac{5}{8} \times 2\frac{15}{16}$ ins.

46. THE WITCH INVIDIOSA RELEASES FANTASIO FROM A CHEST. $5\frac{3}{8} \times 2\frac{15}{16}$ ins.

47. FANTASIO CHANGED INTO A LAPDOG AND ADMITTED INTO DONNA THERESA'S BEDCHAMBER. $5\frac{3}{8} \times 2\frac{15}{16}$ ins.
Two rococo features of the parody are that Fantasio is a boy and is changed into a lapdog and not an ass.

48. CUPID AND PSYCHE. $5\frac{1}{2} \times 2\frac{15}{16}$ ins.

49. DONNA ANGELA HOLDS THE LAPDOG (FANTASIO) WHILE THE CARDINAL INTERROGATES A HERMIT. Second state. $5\frac{3}{8} \times 3$ ins.

50. FRONTISPIECE TO ANTHONY HORNECK'S 'HAPPY ASCETICK'. 1724. $6 \times 3\frac{1}{4}$ ins. British Museum.
A copy of the frontispiece by N. Yeates to the first edition of 1681, with additions.

51. THE MYSTERY OF MASONRY BROUGHT TO LIGHT BY THE GORMOGONS. 1724. Etching and engraving. Third state. Signed. $8\frac{1}{2} \times 13\frac{1}{2}$ ins. British Museum.
The Order of Gormogons, who claimed to have been founded by the first Emperor of China, was a society for ridiculing freemasonry. Hogarth shows both Gormogons and Freemasons issuing from the Grapes Tavern, a lodge of the Freemasons in Westminster. Don Quixote, Sancho Panza and other figures are borrowed from Coypel's *Don Quixote's Adventure at the Puppet Show*. Masonic rites and paraphernalia are caricatured in an indecently ludicrous procession of dupes.

52. ROYALTY, EPISCOPACY AND LAW. 1724. Etching and engraving. $7\frac{3}{16} \times 7\frac{1}{4}$ ins. British Museum.
A telescopic view of the Moon, satirizing the Court. The king's courtiers are his mirrors, his soldiers are fire-screens, and a guinea (bribery), a jew's harp (sanctimonious sermonizing) and a mallet (coercion) take the place of the faces of king, bishop and judge respectively.

53. A JUST VIEW OF THE BRITISH STAGE. December 1724. Second state. $6\frac{15}{16} \times 8\frac{5}{16}$ ins. British Museum.
A further satire on the mania for pantomime, occasioned by the performance of John Thurmond's *Harlequin Shepherd* at Drury Lane, 28 November 1724. Thurmond, who had written the first version of *Harlequin Dr Faustus* in 1723, followed this up with a second pantomime based on the life of the thief Jack Shepherd, who escaped from Newgate Prison four times before being hanged before 200,000 spectators at Tyburn in 1724.

The three managers of the Theatre Royal in Drury Lane, Robert Wilks, Colley Cibber and Barton Booth, plot various pantomimes of a sensational nature, while Tragedy and Comedy are shown disgraced.

54–8. FIVE FRONTISPIECES FOR SIR CHARLES COTTERELL'S TRANSLATION OF 'CASSANDRA' BY LA CALPRENÈDE. 3rd edition, 1725. Etching and engraving. All are signed. British Museum.

54. FRONTISPIECE, Vol. I. $5\frac{1}{16} \times 2\frac{7}{8}$ ins.

55. FRONTISPIECE, Vol. II. $5\frac{1}{8} \times 2\frac{15}{16}$ ins.

56. FRONTISPIECE, Vol. III. $5\frac{1}{8} \times 2\frac{15}{16}$ ins.

57. FRONTISPIECE, Vol. IV. $5\frac{3}{16} \times 2\frac{7}{8}$ ins.

58. FRONTISPIECE, Vol. V. $5\frac{1}{16} \times 2\frac{7}{8}$ ins.

59. A BURLESQUE ON WILLIAM KENT'S ALTARPIECE AT ST CLEMENT DANES. October 1725. Etching. 11 × 7 ins. British Museum.

In 1725, the Bishop of London authorized the removal of Kent's altarpiece, one of the objections being an alleged likeness to the Pretender's wife, Princess Sobieski, and her son. Hogarth seized the opportunity to attack the favourite painter of the Burlington circle for incompetent draughtsmanship.

The key reads:

1. It is not the Pretender's wife and children as our weak brethren imagine.

2. Nor St Cecilia as the connoisseurs think but a choir of angels playing in concert.

A: an organ. B: an angel playing on it. C: the shortest joint of the arm. D: the longest joint. E: an angel tuning a harp. F: the inside of his leg but whether right or left is yet undiscovered. G: a hand playing on a lute. H: the other leg judiciously omitted to make room for the harp. I and K: smaller angels as appears by their wings.

60–1. TWO ILLUSTRATIONS FOR JOHN MILTON'S 'PARADISE LOST'. *c.* 1725. Both signed. Royal Library, Windsor Castle.
In the style of Callot. Possibly rejected illustrations for the Tonson edition of 1725.

60. THE COUNCIL IN HELL (Book II). Signed. $5\frac{1}{8} \times 2\frac{15}{16}$ ins.

61. THE COUNCIL IN HEAVEN (Book III). Signed. $5\frac{5}{16} \times 2\frac{15}{16}$ ins.

62–75. FOURTEEN ILLUSTRATIONS FOR JOHN BEAVER'S 'ROMAN MILITARY PUNISHMENTS'. 1725. Etchings. All are signed except the frontispiece. The text contrasts the rigour of the Republic with the cruelty of the Emperors. Again influenced by Callot. British Museum.

62. FRONTISPIECE. A seated Roman general on a camp stool. $2\frac{1}{16} \times 2\frac{3}{16}$ ins.

63. FUSTIGATIO, OR BEATING TO DEATH WITH STICKS AND CUDGELS. $1\frac{1}{2} \times 2\frac{13}{16}$ ins.

64. DECIMATION. $1\frac{7}{16} \times 2\frac{13}{16}$ ins.

65. BEHEADING. $1\frac{1}{2} \times 2\frac{13}{16}$ ins.

66. CRUCIFIXION, etc. $1\frac{9}{16} \times 2\frac{7}{8}$ ins.

67. DISMEMBERMENT, etc. $1\frac{1}{2} \times 2\frac{13}{16}$ ins.
This shows tearing apart by releasing branches of trees, being bound to a wagon and being sewn alive in the bellies of oxen.

68. FREEMEN DEGRADED AND SOLD INTO SLAVERY. $1\frac{3}{8} \times 2\frac{3}{4}$ ins.
A punishment for avoiding military duty.

69. BANISHMENT. $1\frac{3}{8} \times 2\frac{3}{4}$ ins.

70. BREAKING THE LEGS. $1\frac{1}{2} \times 2\frac{3}{4}$ ins.

71. FUSTIUM ADMONITIO. $1\frac{1}{2} \times 2\frac{3}{4}$ ins.
A lighter beating for negligence of duty.

72. SHAMEFUL DISCHARGE. $1\frac{1}{2} \times 2\frac{13}{16}$ ins.

73. TAKING AWAY THE MILITARY BELT OR GIRDLE. $1\frac{1}{2} \times 2\frac{13}{16}$ ins.

74. DEGRADING PUNISHMENTS. $1\frac{1}{2} \times 2\frac{3}{4}$ ins.
The offenders march among captives with the baggage, after their spears have been taken away and broken.

75. ISSUED BARLEY INSTEAD OF WHEAT. First version. $1\frac{1}{2} \times 2\frac{3}{4}$ ins.
Barley was the food of beasts of burden.

76–7. TWO ILLUSTRATIONS FOR A PROPOSED SEQUEL ON 'MODERN MILITARY PUNISHMENTS'. Etching. Both signed. British Museum.
This was never published.

76. CUTTING OFF THE NOSE. $1\frac{1}{2} \times 2\frac{7}{8}$ ins.

77. HANGING BY THE THUMBS. $1\frac{1}{2} \times 2\frac{7}{8}$ ins.

78. ABRAHAM BUYS A FIELD FROM EPHRON THE HITTITE. *c.* 1725. Etching and engraving. $5\frac{3}{8} \times 3\frac{1}{2}$ ins. British Museum. Attributed to Hogarth. Probably for a book, as yet unidentified.

79–95. SEVENTEEN SMALL BOOK ILLUSTRATIONS FOR SAMUEL BUTLER'S 'HUDIBRAS'. Before April 1726. Etching and engraving. All are signed. University of Illinois, except frontispiece.
Butler's poem *Hudibras*, first published in parts from 1662 to 1678, and based on Cervantes' *Don Quixote*, was the classic satire on the Puritans from the point of view of the Royalist Party. Although the edition that Hogarth illustrated was not published until April 1726, there can be little doubt that they are earlier than the *Large Illustrations* advertised as a separate set in October 1725. The latter are entirely his own invention, while the small illustrations are freely based on anonymous illustrations in an edition of *Hudibras* first published in 1710.

79. FRONTISPIECE: HEAD OF SAMUEL BUTLER. $3\frac{7}{8} \times 2\frac{3}{4}$ ins. Bodleian Library, Oxford.
Actually a copy of John White's mezzotint of the portrait of the painter Jean-Baptiste Monnoyer.

80. HUDIBRAS SALLYING FORTH. Part I, Canto I. $4\frac{3}{4} \times 2\frac{13}{16}$ ins.

81. HUDIBRAS' FIRST ADVENTURE. Part I, Canto II. $4\frac{1}{2} \times 4\frac{15}{16}$ ins.

82. HUDIBRAS ENCOUNTERING TALGOL AND MAGNANO. Part I, Canto II. $4\frac{5}{16} \times 4\frac{15}{16}$ ins.

83. TRULLA ATTACKING HUDIBRAS. Part I, Canto III. $4\frac{5}{8} \times 2\frac{3}{4}$ ins.

84. HUDIBRAS VANQUISHED BY TRULLA. Part I, Canto III. $4\frac{3}{4} \times 2\frac{7}{8}$ ins.

85. HUDIBRAS AND RALPHO CARRIED TO THE STOCKS. Part I, Canto III. $4\frac{1}{8} \times 5$ ins.

86. HUDIBRAS AND RALPHO DISPUTING. Part I, Canto III. $4\frac{5}{8} \times 2\frac{7}{8}$ ins.

87. HUDIBRAS VISITED BY THE WIDOW. Part II, Canto I. $4\frac{9}{16} \times 2\frac{3}{4}$ ins.

88. HUDIBRAS AND THE SKIMMINGTON. Part II, Canto II. $4\frac{9}{16} \times 9\frac{1}{2}$ ins. See No. 103.

89. SIDROPHEL EXAMINING THE KITE THROUGH HIS TELESCOPE. Part II, Canto III. $4\frac{9}{16} \times 2\frac{11}{16}$ ins.

90. HUDIBRAS VISITING SIDROPHEL. Part II, Canto III. $4\frac{5}{8} \times 2\frac{3}{4}$ ins.

91. HUDIBRAS BEATING SIDROPHEL AND WHACUM. Part II, Canto III. $4\frac{5}{8} \times 2\frac{3}{4}$ ins.

92. HUDIBRAS WOOING THE WIDOW. Part III, Canto I. $4\frac{9}{16} \times 2\frac{11}{16}$ ins.

93. HUDIBRAS CATECHIZED. Part III, Canto I. $4\frac{1}{2} \times 2\frac{11}{16}$ ins.

94. BURNING THE RUMPS AT TEMPLE BAR. Part III, Canto II. $4\frac{3}{16} \times 5$ ins.

95. HUDIBRAS AND THE LAWYER. Part III, Canto II. $4\frac{5}{8} \times 2\frac{3}{16}$ ins.

96. FRONTISPIECE TO NICHOLAS AMHURST'S 'TERRAE-FILIUS, OR THE SECRET HISTORY OF THE UNIVERSITY OF OXFORD'. Signed. $5\frac{5}{16} \times 3\frac{1}{16}$ ins. British Museum.
A Fellow of Oxford is expelled for writing a lampoon on a lady.

97–108. TWELVE LARGE ILLUSTRATIONS FOR SAMUEL BUTLER'S 'HUDIBRAS'. February 1725/6. Etching and engraving. British Museum.

97. FRONTISPIECE. First state. Signed. $9\frac{9}{16} \times 13\frac{11}{16}$ ins.
The bas-relief shows Butler's genius lashing Hypocrisy, Ignorance and Rebellion in a car pulled round Mount Parnassus by Hudibras and Ralpho. Britannia looks into the truthful Mirror of Nature.

97.*FRONTISPIECE. Drawing for the engraving, in reverse. Pencil, with grey-black ink, brown and grey washes; incised. $9\frac{1}{2} \times 13\frac{3}{8}$ ins. Royal Library, Windsor Castle.

Note that in the print the satyr is replaced by Britannia, and that the tomb of Butler behind the satyr has been altered.

98. HUDIBRAS SALLIES FORTH. Part I, Canto I. Second state. $9\frac{7}{8} \times 13\frac{3}{8}$ ins.

99. HUDIBRAS' FIRST ADVENTURE. Part I, Canto I. Second state. Signed. $9\frac{3}{4} \times 13\frac{1}{8}$ ins.

100. HUDIBRAS TRIUMPHANT. Part I, Canto II. First state. $9\frac{3}{4} \times 13\frac{3}{8}$ ins.

101. HUDIBRAS VANQUISHED BY TRULLA. Part I, Canto III. Second state. $9\frac{7}{16} \times 13\frac{5}{16}$ ins.

102. HUDIBRAS IN TRIBULATION. Part II, Canto I. Second state. $9\frac{11}{16} \times 13\frac{1}{2}$ ins.

103. HUDIBRAS AND THE SKIMMINGTON. Part II, Canto III. First state. $9\frac{3}{4} \times 19\frac{15}{16}$ ins.

The Skimmington was a rural English custom for punishing shrews and henpecked husbands, who were tied together on a horse and escorted through the village in a public procession.

The composition is a parody of Annibale Carracci's *Procession of Bacchus and Ariadne* in the Farnese Palace, Rome.

104. HUDIBRAS BEATS SIDROPHEL AND WHACUM. Part II, Canto III. First state. $9\frac{3}{4} \times 13\frac{11}{16}$ ins.

A learned satire on quacks, astrologers and necromancy. The books on the shelf refer to Pliny's *Natural History*, a popular work on magic ascribed to Merlin and Jean Bodin's *De la démonamie des sorciers* (1580).

105. HUDIBRAS CATECHIZED. Part III, Canto I. Second state. $9\frac{3}{4} \times 13\frac{5}{8}$ ins.

106. THE COMMITTEE. Part III, Canto II. First state. $9\frac{5}{8} \times 13\frac{3}{8}$ ins.

107. BURNING THE RUMPS AT TEMPLE BAR. Part III, Canto II. Second state. Signed. $9\frac{13}{16} \times 19\frac{3}{4}$ ins.

To protest against the Rump Parliament in power after Cromwell's death, a London mob took rumps of beef from the butchers' shops and roasted them in the street, crying 'No more Rump'.

108. HUDIBRAS AND THE LAWYER. Part III, Canto III. Second state. Signed. $9\frac{3}{8} \times 13\frac{11}{16}$ ins.

109–10. TWO PLATES FOR JOHN BLACKWELL'S 'COMPENDIUM OF MILITARY DISCIPLINE'. 1726. Etching and engraving. British Museum.

These were folding diagrams to accompany the text, for use as a manual by the six regiments of the City of London Militia. Influenced by Callot's *Excercices militaires*.

109. EXERCISE FOR THE HALBERD. $12\frac{7}{8} \times 19\frac{3}{4}$ ins.

110. MANUAL FOR SALUTING WITH THE HALF-PIKE. $12\frac{3}{4} \times 22\frac{7}{8}$ ins.

111. LETTERHEAD FOR BLUNDELL'S SCHOOL, TIVERTON. September 1726. Signed. $4\frac{3}{8} \times 5\frac{3}{4}$ ins. British Museum.

An invitation to a reunion of *alumni*. Minerva points to the school, while Mercury performs the rôle of Grammatica watering a young plant.

112. CUNICULARII, OR THE WISE MEN OF GODLIMAN IN CONSULTATION. December 1726. Etching. $6\frac{5}{16} \times 9\frac{7}{16}$ ins. British Museum.

Mary Tofts, an illiterate woman of Godalming, Surrey, caused a sensation in 1726 by claiming to have given birth to a number of rabbits at the rate of one a day. Eminent doctors came from London to verify this remarkable event, which caused a temporary decline in the consumption of rabbits and hares at the dinner table. Mrs Tofts eventually confessed to fraud.

The characters are (A) Nathaniel St André, Anatomist to the Royal Household, (B) Dr Sir Richard Manningham, (C) Dr Cyriacus Ahlers, (D) Dr John Howard, the local doctor who claimed to have delivered the first rabbits, (E) Joshua Tofts the husband, (F) Mary Tofts and (G) the Nurse. D at the door rejects a rabbit offered by a game-dealer and gives as his reason, 'It's too big.'

113. THE PUNISHMENT INFLICTED ON LEMUEL GULLIVER. December 1726. Etching and engraving. First state. Signed. $7\frac{7}{16} \times 12\frac{1}{8}$ ins. British Museum.

Hogarth came out with this print almost immediately after Swift's *Gulliver's Travels* was published, and jokingly claimed that it was the original frontispiece, left out by accident. The mock engraver's name 'Nathanoi Tfiws' is an anagram of Jonathan Swift.

Gulliver had put out a fire in the Royal Palace at Lilliput by urinating, and is now being ignominiously punished with a fire-engine. The moral is that court and country do not always understand those ministers who have sometimes to adopt drastic and unpopular measures.

114. MASQUERADE TICKET. 1727. $7\frac{3}{16} \times 10$ ins. British Museum.

On the appointment of the Swiss, Heidegger, as Master of the King's Revels, Hogarth published this print depicting a party of masqueraders in the interior of the King's Theatre, Haymarket. On the left is the altar of Priapus before which a bishop and a butcher 'kill' Time. On the right is the altar of the masked Venus, who looks at two 'Lechero-meters'. The Royal Lion and Unicorn on the clock have completely abandoned any attempt to maintain their heraldic dignity.

115. MUSIC INTRODUCED TO APOLLO BY MINERVA. *c.* 1727. Etching and engraving. First state. Signed. $7\frac{3}{4} \times 8\frac{1}{2}$ ins. British Museum.

The arms are those of John Manners, 3rd Duke of Rutland, a patron of Handel, whose music Hogarth greatly admired.

116. MUSIC INTRODUCED TO APOLLO BY MINERVA. *c.* 1727. Etching and engraving. Third state. Signed. $9\frac{7}{16} \times 6\frac{3}{16}$ ins. British Museum.

117. FRONTISPIECE TO RICHARD LEVERIDGE'S 'COLLECTION OF SONGS', 1727. November 1727. Etching and engraving. First state. $6\frac{7}{16} \times 3\frac{7}{8}$ ins. British Museum.

The Muse of the composer appeals to Bacchus and Venus, who is solicited by Cupid.

118. FRONTISPIECE TO THOMAS COOKE'S TRANSLATION OF HESIOD. February 1727/8. Signed. $6\frac{9}{16} \times 4\frac{3}{8}$ ins. British Museum.

119. BENEFIT TICKET FOR THE ACTOR WILLIAM MILWARD. April 1728. Etching. $3\frac{7}{16} \times 4\frac{1}{16}$ ins. Royal Library, Windsor Castle.

The actor is shown in a scene from John Gay's *Beggar's Opera*, a play greatly admired by Hogarth for its realism and wit.

120. HENRY VIII AND ANNE BOLYN. *c.* 1728/9. Etching and engraving. First state. $17\frac{5}{8} \times 14\frac{5}{16}$ ins. British Museum.

This print was occasioned by the success of Colley Cibber's production of Shakespeare's *Henry VIII* in 1727, and by the polemical identification of Cardinal Wolsey and Sir Robert Walpole as bad ministers.

121–2. TWO ILLUSTRATIONS FOR 'PERSEUS AND ANDROMEDA', A VERSE DRAMA BY LEWIS THEOBALD, 1730. 1730/1. British Museum.

121. FRONTISPIECE: PERSEUS SLAYING MEDUSA. Signed. 6×4 ins.

122. PERSEUS RESCUING ANDROMEDA. Signed. $5\frac{15}{16} \times 4\frac{1}{8}$ ins.

123. FOUR HEADS FROM THE RAPHAEL CARTOONS AT HAMPTON COURT. *c.* 1730. Etching. First state. $8\frac{7}{16} \times 14$ ins. British Museum.

Published posthumously by the widow of the artist. After 1729, Sir James Thornhill made copies of the Raphael cartoons, and these etchings may have been done by his son-in-law for a proposed publication of details for the use of students.

124. SANCHO'S FEAST. *c.* 1730. Etching and engraving. Third state. Signed. $10\frac{7}{8} \times 11\frac{9}{16}$ ins. British Museum.

A commission from Henry Overton and John Hoole, who specialized in *Don Quixote* illustrations and had published the first English edition of the set by Coypel. Influenced by the Raphael cartoons.

125. FRONTISPIECE TO THE 'HUMOURS OF OXFORD', A COMEDY BY JAMES MILLER. April 1730. Etching and engraving by G. Vandergucht after a design from the life by Hogarth. $6\frac{1}{2} \times 4\frac{1}{8}$ ins. British Museum.

A drunken Fellow shocks the Vice-Chancellor of his University.

126. FRONTISPIECE TO 'THE TRAVELS OF MR. JOHN GULLIVER' BY P. F. G. DESFONTAINES. February 1730/1. Etching and engraving by G. Vandergucht after Hogarth's design. $5\frac{3}{16} \times 2\frac{13}{16}$ ins. British Museum.

Gulliver infatuates the Amazonian Queen of Babilary.

127. FRONTISPIECE TO HENRY FIELDING'S 'TRAGEDY OF TRAGEDIES'. March 1730/1. Etched and engraved by G. Vandergucht after Hogarth's design. $6\frac{3}{16} \times 3\frac{11}{16}$ ins. British Museum.
The Princess Humcamunca and the Amazon Glumdalca quarrel over Tom Thumb, in parody of Octavia and Cleopatra in Dryden's *All for Love* (Act II, scene vii).

128. FRONTISPIECE TO 'THE HIGHLAND FAIR', A BALLAD-OPERA BY JOSEPH MITCHELL. March 1730/1. Etching and engraving by G. Vandergucht after Hogarth's design. $6 \times 3\frac{13}{16}$ ins. British Museum.

129. TASTE, OR BURLINGTON GATE. December–January 1731/2. Engraving, attributed to Hogarth. $8\frac{3}{8} \times 6\frac{1}{4}$ ins. British Museum.
The caption reads: (A) a Plasterer whitewashing and bespattering (B) any Body that comes his way. (C) not a Duke's coach as appears by the crescent at one corner. (D) Taste. (E) a standing Proof. (F) a Labourer.
A is Alexander Pope, B the Duke of Chandos and E the ineffable William Kent, who once again receives the admiring glances of Raphael and Michelangelo on the gateway to Burlington House.
Pope, whose *Epistle of Taste* was dedicated to Lord Burlington, did not reply to this attack, the only recorded instance of his refusing a challenge. Perhaps as a hunchback he feared the artist more than he did men of letters.
Hogarth seems to have deliberately chosen a somewhat primitive style to ridicule the puppet-like character of his victims.

130. BOYS PEEPING AT NATURE. 1730/1. Etching. Second state. $3\frac{1}{2} \times 4\frac{3}{4}$ ins. Royal Library, Windsor Castle.
A subscription ticket for *The Harlot's Progress*, and as such a manifesto of his artistic intentions in introducing a new art form. Nature is the many-breasted mother of the arts. An Infant Genius rushes to restrain a satyr from exploring her indecent parts. The noble and indecent approaches to Nature justify the licence of the moral satirist, who has to expose the realities of life.
Sir James Thornhill, the father-in-law with whom Hogarth was not reconciled, possessed the Rubens–Jan Brueghel *Nature Adorned by the Graces*, now in the Glasgow Art Gallery, showing the many-breasted torso of Nature.

130.*BOYS PEEPING AT NATURE. Drawing for the engraving (first state) in reverse. Pencil and grey wash, touched with pen and black ink; incised in places. $4 \times 5\frac{1}{4}$ ins. Royal Library, Windsor Castle.

131. BOYS PEEPING AT NATURE. 1751. Etching. Fourth state. $3\frac{1}{2} \times 4\frac{3}{4}$ ins. British Museum.
Hogarth continued to use the design for a subscription ticket, on this occasion for *Moses brought to Pharaoh's Daughter*, and *Paul before Felix* (1751). Because these were history paintings, and therefore ideal, the satyr has been omitted, as well as the quotations from Virgil and Horace.

132. A WOMAN SWEARING A CHILD TO A GRAVE CITIZEN. After 1729. Etching and engraving by Joseph Sympson Jr. $10\frac{1}{16} \times 13\frac{1}{4}$ ins. British Museum.
This atrocious print must be included because it bears Hogarth's signature as the painter and may have been authorized by him to help Sympson, with whose father he had studied at the St Martin's Lane Academy. Hogarth's original painting is in the National Gallery of Ireland, Dublin.
A young woman in pregnancy swears that the sober citizen with hands upraised is the father of her child, while she is prompted by her real lover.

133. ORATOR HENLEY CHRISTENING A CHILD. After 1729. Mezzotint. Signed by J. Sympson Jr. $11\frac{3}{8} \times 15\frac{3}{4}$ ins. Royal Library, Windsor Castle.
If anything, worse than the former. Again after an authentic painting. Hogarth's name does not appear, so that it may not have been authorized.
John 'Orator' Henley had broken with the Church of England and set up on his own as a preacher who attracted a following of dupes by his showmanship. The husband, Sir Fopling, looks in the mirror but does not see the young man paying court to his wife. The quack clergyman is more interested in one of the young ladies than the infant he is supposed to be baptizing. The Holy Water is being spilled on the floor.
The prints are interesting because they illustrate ideas which Hogarth developed in his later work.

134–9. A HARLOT'S PROGRESS. April 1732. 6 plates. Etching and engraving. All signed. British Museum. The original paintings were destroyed by the fire at Fonthill in 1755.

134. PLATE I. First state. $11\frac{13}{16} \times 14\frac{3}{4}$ ins.
The characters are an innocent country girl (Moll Hackabout), a bawd (the notorious Mother Needham), a lecher (the infamous Colonel Francis Chartres, who died after a lifetime of vice, just before the series appeared) and a country clergyman.

So obsessive was the appetite of Colonel Chartres for fresh young women that he employed panders, one of whom stands beside him, at inns where coaches arrived from the country. Here he is forestalled by Mother Needham, who presents herself as a fine lady needing a servant.

A goose in a basket is addressed to 'my loving cousin in Thames Street'. The cousin has failed to arrive. The clergyman, who has accompanied the wagon from York, thus stands *in loco parentis*, but is too busy reading the address of a Bishop (from whom he expects preferment) to notice the seduction. He also overlooks the prophetic disaster his hungry horse is about to bring about.

135. THE QUARREL WITH HER JEW PROTECTOR. Plate II. First state. $11\frac{7}{8} \times 14\frac{5}{8}$ ins.

Moll has risen from employment in Mother Needham's brothel to become the mistress of a rich Jew, who has installed her in a luxurious apartment. He calls unexpectedly in the morning. She serves tea, but the young lover whom she has acquired at a masquerade ball (see the mask on the dressing table) is still hiding in the bed. To ensure his escape, she upsets the table in an assumed fit of temper. Assisted by her maid, the young man, with his breeches hastily pulled on, creeps unnoticed out of the room.

The monkey and the blackamoor page illustrate the expensive fads of the harlot, the pictures on the wall the taste of the Jew. They are Old Testament subjects with a lesson which he has yet to learn. Jonah sits beside his gourd, which sprang up in the night and was withered by the worm in the morning. Uzzah reaches for the Ark of the Covenant, but is struck dead by God for his offence. In the same picture the angry wife of David watches him dancing from a window. The general theme of retribution is equally applicable to Jew and mistress.

136. APPREHENDED BY A MAGISTRATE. Plate III. First state. $10\frac{13}{16} \times 14\frac{7}{8}$ ins.

Once again we see Moll taking morning tea, but in very different circumstances. Cast aside by the Jew, she has become a common prostitute in Drury Lane. She still has both a lover, the highwayman James Dalton, whose wig-box rests above the bed, and a servant, this time a repulsive one.

Nearly all the imagery and accessories correspond to those in the previous picture. The cat replaces the monkey, prints of Captain MacHeath, the highwayman hero of *The Beggar's Opera*, and Dr Sacheveral, the political favourite of the mob, are substituted for the paintings of Jonah and Uzzah. The stolen watch shows that the harlot has remained expert in deceiving those who pay for her favours.

Mr Justice Gonson, notorious for his harlot-hunting zeal, arrives with his bailiffs to make an arrest. Two medicine bottles and an ointment pot, above the portrait of Sacheveral, forecast a more terrible retribution than prison.

The knotted bed-curtain suggests, almost compulsively, a tragic mask.

137. SCENE IN BRIDEWELL. Plate IV. First state. $11\frac{7}{8} \times 14\frac{15}{16}$ ins.

Moll beats hemp in Bridewell Prison next to a gentleman in a handsome coat. A torn playing card in front of him indicates the cause of his downfall. The leering gaoler's wife fingers the harlot's fine clothes, which will become hers when the young woman breaks down and purchases a temporary respite from the severity of her tormentor.

While she keeps her fine clothes, Moll will remain at the upper-class end of the shed, with the cardsharper and the young gentleman in the stocks. By contrast, her servant sits next to a slut who is destroying vermin.

On the shutter at the back is an effigy of Sir John Gonson hanging from the gallows, a macabre reminder of one of the uses to be made from the hemp that the prisoners are making.

138. SHE EXPIRES, WHILE THE DOCTORS ARE QUARRELLING. Plate V. First state. $12 \times 14\frac{3}{4}$ ins.

Again the symbol of a table occupies the centre of the stage. It has fallen to the ground, and its contents are smashed. The harlot expires, attended by her faithful servant. Two quack doctors, identified as Dr Richard Rock and Dr Jean Misaubin, quarrel about their respective medicines. Venereal disease was frequently cured in the eighteenth century, and this print may have promoted a well-known joke, more common on the Continent than in England, 'Cause of death – two doctors'.

The shocked remonstrance of the waiting-woman highlights the indifference of the others: the quarrelling doctors, the old woman who has come to prepare the corpse and is going through the trunks, and the son scratching his head while toasting his supper. A reminder of her Jewish keeper is the Jewish mazzo cake used as a fly-trap above the door.

139. THE FUNERAL. Plate VI. First state. $11\frac{13}{16} \times 14\frac{7}{8}$ ins.

A Drury Lane confraternity is shown mourning the deceased harlot. The corrupt clergyman and the undertaker react in different ways to the attractions of the opposite sex. Grief and demonstrations of piety are chiefly stimulated by alcohol. The handsome young woman in the centre is merely curious to inspect the corpse. Another woman admires herself in the mirror. The faithful servant is as shocked by the conduct of the parson as she was by that of the doctors. The boy, handsomely clad as chief mourner, plays unconcernedly with a peg-top.

140. A CHORUS OF SINGERS. December 1732. Etching. First state. $6\frac{9}{16} \times 6\frac{1}{8}$ ins. British Museum.

Used as a subscription ticket for *A Midnight Modern Conversation*, it depicts a rehearsal of the oratorio *Judith* by Hogarth's friend William Huggins, with music by William Defesch, performed 16 February 1732/3 at Lincoln's Inn Fields.

141. A MIDNIGHT MODERN CONVERSATION. March 1732/3. Etching and engraving. First state. Signed. 12$\frac{15}{16}$ × 18 ins. British Museum.
The scene is St John's Coffee House, Temple Bar, and the time four o'clock in the morning. In eighteenth-century England the word 'conversation' was also used for a party – a tea party, fishing party, hunting party, etc. – and this is quite simply a drinking party. The group consists of well-known tavern personalities, who have been identified as Parson Cornelius Ford, the disreputable cousin of Dr Johnson, who is ladling punch; the tobacconist John Harrison, popular for his songs, who puts his wig on the parson's head; on his right, Kettleby, a boisterous barrister; the bookbinder Chandler who worked for Hogarth, in a white night cap; another friend of Hogarth, a doctor, shown pouring wine on James Figg the prizefighter, whom only Bacchus could knock out. The figure on the right has the *London Journal* and the *Craftsman* in his pocket, showing that he is a politician. While thinking about politics, he sets fire to his ruffle.
The print is a parody of Dutch tavern scenes by Jan Steen, Jordaens and others, perhaps with a sly allusion to more elevated Dutch group portraits by Hals and Rembrandt, as suggested by Paulson.

142. SARAH MALCOLM. March 1732/3. Etching and engraving. Signed. 7 × 7 ins. British Museum.
Hogarth and his father-in-law Sir James Thornhill visited Sarah Malcolm, a handsome charwoman who murdered her mistress and her companion for money, a few days before her execution. The print sold rapidly but was promptly pirated.

143–4. TWO ILLUSTRATIONS TO MOLIÈRE. Etching and engraving by G. Vandergucht after Hogarth's design. Both in British Museum.
Frontispiece to the two plays making up the first volume of *Selected Comedies of Mr. de Molière*, 8 vols, London, 1732.

143. FRONTISPIECE TO 'L'AVARE'. Second state. 5 × 3$\frac{1}{16}$ ins.
Harpagon the miser snuffs out a candle, because one is sufficient.

144. FRONTISPIECE TO 'SGANARELLE OU LE COCU IMAGINAIRE'. Second state. 5$\frac{1}{16}$ × 3$\frac{1}{8}$ ins.
Sganarelle makes the cuckold's sign on discovering his wife with a miniature portrait of a young man, although she has picked it up by accident.

145. FRONTISPIECE TO THE ORATORIO 'JUDITH'. 1733. Etching and engraving, by G. Vandergucht, after Hogarth's design. 5$\frac{11}{16}$ × 3$\frac{1}{16}$ ins. British Museum.
For the publication of William Huggins' work (see No. 140).

146. THE LAUGHING AUDIENCE. December 1733. Etching. First state. 7 × 6$\frac{1}{4}$ ins. Fitzwilliam Museum, Cambridge.
Used as a subscription ticket for *Southwark Fair* and *A Rake's Progress*. The orchestra in the theatre is protected from the commoners in the pit by a row of spikes. The performance is hugely enjoyed except by a disgusted critic (at that time critics sat in the pit) and two foppish gentlemen who rudely pay no attention because they have found other interests.

147. SOUTHWARK FAIR. January 1733/4. Etching and engraving. Signed. 13$\frac{1}{2}$ × 17$\frac{13}{16}$ ins. British Museum.
A congeries of actors, acrobats, showmen, prizefighters, musicians, conjurors and gamesters, the majority of whom are trying to attract an audience inside the booth, tavern or other building in which their performances will be held. Nearly all the allusions are specific and topical, and refer to popular entertainments, well-known personalities of the stage and quarrels in the world of the theatre.
At both Bartholomew and Southwark Fairs the leading stage companies competed for the favours of the public against the competition of peepshows, Punch and Judy, etc.
The central theme of the satire has been aptly defined by Paulson as the 'Fall' motif, connected with the discrepancy between appearance and reality. The sign of the *Fall of Troy* dominates the scene, and the actors below it advertise, among other performances, the *Fall of Phaeton*. The sign of *The Stage Mutiny* copies a lampoon by John Laguerre on the troubles of the Drury Lane company after its take-over by Highmore. In the centre we witness the downfall of a Roman emperor arrested by a bailiff. The tight-rope walker and rope-flyer run the same risk. The Fall of Adam and Eve is alluded to in the sign beneath the flag. Under this is depicted the downfall of Joan, wheeled by Punch into Hell-mouth. The actors advertising the *Fall of Bajazet* literally fall down onto a china shop as their stage collapses. The list can be extended by studying the episodes among the crowd, notably the young girls being decoyed by an artful villain.
In the centre two country yokels admire a drummer-girl, a symbol of the contradiction between illusion and reality.

148–63. THE RAKE'S PROGRESS. June 1735. 8 plates. Etching and engraving. All are from the British Museum, except where otherwise stated.

The series was held back until the Copyright Act, popularly known as Hogarth's Act, became law in June 1735. Because the prints were so popular and protected by copyright, he now had an incentive to improve the later states. Two states are therefore shown throughout for comparison, so valuable for understanding the way in which his imagination worked. Hogarth sometimes changes shading, the faces, the detail, adds inscriptions and accessories and in Plate IV a whole group of figures.

148–9. THE YOUNG HEIR TAKES POSSESSION OF THE MISER'S EFFECTS. Plate I. First and third states. Signed. $12\frac{9}{16} \times 15\frac{3}{8}$ ins.

A rich merchant has died and his heir, Tom Rakewell, is being measured for a suit of mourning. He is interrupted by Mrs Young and her pregnant daughter Sarah, whom he seduced with a promise of marriage while a student at Oxford (see the ring and address on a letter). He now offers to buy her off.

A workman who is hanging the room with black mourning cloth discovers a hidden hoard of money. A painting in the Dutch style hangs over the mantelpiece. It shows a merchant counting and weighing money, and can be identified as a portrait of the deceased by the fur cap below. The signs of miserliness are everywhere, and include a candle-saver on the mantelpiece, a cupboard with a collection of old wigs, old boots, etc., a chest filled with plate and money-bags, and a diary with the entry 'Put off my bad shilling'. An old servant, freed from the surveillance of her master, prepares a generous fire. The steward or lawyer notices that the heir has not counted the handful of guineas he has taken from the bag, and steals some coins behind his back.

Among the many significant changes in the third state, the diary has been put in a more conspicuous position and its place taken by a Bible with its leather binding cut to make the sole of a shoe.

150. SURROUNDED BY ARTISTS AND PROFESSORS. Plate II. First state. Unfinished proof. $12\frac{3}{8} \times 15\frac{1}{4}$ ins. Royal Library, Windsor Castle.

151. SURROUNDED BY ARTISTS AND PROFESSORS. Plate II. Third state. Signed. $12\frac{3}{8} \times 15\frac{1}{4}$ ins.

The Rake's Levee is attended only by sycophants. On one side are grouped a French dancing master with his violin, a landscape gardener (possibly Charles Bridgman), James Figg the prizefighter with his quarter-staffs, and the French fencing master Dubois, killed in a duel on 10 May 1734; and on the other side, a jockey kneeling with a trophy won at Epsom by a horse called 'Silly Tom', a hireling bravo or bully, and a man trying out a hunting horn. The musician at the harpsichord on the left is Niccolo Porpora, who directed the King's Theatre, Haymarket, in opposition to Hogarth's hero Handel. The long scroll contains a list of ridiculous but expensive presents allegedly given by the English nobility and gentry to Farinelli, the famous Italian castrato singer whom Porpora promoted: in the background a short and shrivelled poet reading an 'Epistle to Rake', refers to the practice of Alexander Pope in dedicating epistles to aristocratic patrons.

On the wall *The Judgment of Paris* is hung between two fighting cocks to form a triptych in honour of Beauty attended by Sport.

152. THE TAVERN SCENE. Plate III. Second state. Signed. $12\frac{1}{2} \times 15\frac{1}{4}$ ins.

153. THE TAVERN SCENE. Plate III. Third state. Signed. $12\frac{1}{2} \times 14\frac{1}{4}$ ins.

The Rake and his companion in the Rose Tavern, Drury Lane, after the hero has captured the lantern and staff of a watchman in a street exploit. He is too intoxicated and otherwise distracted to notice that his watch is being stolen. The woman undressing in the right foreground is preparing to perform postures on the platter carried in by a waiter. The bawling of a street-singer advanced in pregnancy competes with the music made by a trumpeter and harpist in the corner. A tipsy girl standing on a chair tries to set fire to a map of the world with a candle. The other pictures are Titian's portraits of the Roman emperors, but the heads have all been cut out, except that of Nero, the most depraved of them all. In the third state, Julius Caesar on the left is replaced by Pontac, a President of the *Parlament* of Bordeaux after whom Pontac's eating-house in Abchurch Lane was named.

The Rake has reached the degenerate stage of Nero, and his own world or empire will shortly be destroyed around him.

154. ARRESTED FOR DEBT. Plate IV. First state. Signed. $12\frac{1}{2} \times 15\frac{1}{4}$ ins.

Fearing his creditors, the Rake has drawn the curtains of his sedan chair on the way to a levee at St James's Palace, the pinnacle of his social career. Nevertheless, he is detected and arrested by two bailiffs. The faithful Sarah Young, now a seamstress, and conveniently on the spot, offers him her savings. The Welshman with a leek in his hat fixes the date as St David's Day, 1 March, the birthday of Queen Caroline.

A lamplighter is so distracted by the arrest that he spills the oil intended for the lamp.

155. ARRESTED FOR DEBT. Plate IV. Third state. Signed. 12½ × 15¼ ins.

The changes in the third state introduced a two-pronged attack on gambling. A bolt of lightning is aimed at White's, a club and gambling house for the aristocracy. On the right a post has been labelled 'Blacks'. Before it a group of street urchins, including shoe-blacks, form a rival club. Each plays his part in a precise parody of his seniors and social superiors, their parasites and their behaviour. The first boy on the left is a student of world affairs, reading *The Farthing Post* and smoking his pipe. The cardplayer in the centre is a newsvendor, also with political interests, for a paper inscribed 'Your Vote & Interest – Libertys' is stuck in his hat. He is being cheated by his opponent, whose accomplice signals the cards that he holds. No doubt he was flattered by the chance to gamble with so grand a person in a full-bottomed wig, a prince among shoe-blacks. A dice-thrower has won all the clothes except his breeches from a shoe-black with a small pot and inverted spirit glass before him. This is a wholly masculine School of Rakes, not a feminine School for Scandal, and not a single member of the club pays the slightest attention to the scandalous catastrophe of the hero, except the one who picks his pocket. The humour of the group is that it can be read, *mutatis mutandis*, as a scene inside White's.

The print is reminiscent of Claude Gillot's *Scène des carrosses* in the Louvre.

156. MARRIED TO AN OLD MAID. Plate V. First state. Signed. 12⁷⁄₁₆ × 15⅜ ins.

157. MARRIED TO AN OLD MAID. Plate V. Third state. Signed. 12⁷⁄₁₆ × 15⅜ ins.

To recoup his fortunes, Tom marries an old, one-eyed heiress in Mary-le-bone Old Church, notorious for secret weddings outside town, while the pew-opener tries to prevent Sarah Young, her mother and her child by the Rake from stopping the ceremony.

The key to the meaning of the print is the tablet of the second half of the Ten Commandments, all of which are devoted to 'Duties to our Neighbours'. Each is cracked except the last, 'Thou shall not covet . . . thy neighbour's . . . maid.' The Rake already has his eye on the bride's servant, who is about to become his own in more senses than one. A vigorous dog gallantly addresses, in loyal emulation of his master, a one-eyed bitch.

The Creed is so rotted that only 'I believe' is legible. The poor-box is covered by a large cobweb. The spider has chosen the place in the church where it is safest from disturbance. An inscription on the balcony states that the church was 'beautified' in 1725. Either the churchwardens have cheated the parish, or the church has been sadly neglected. The evergreen decorations allude to Lust and Winter, that is, to the passions and attractions of the bride.

Hogarth has made an interesting change in the third state. In the first state the innocent face of the bridesmaid accidentally resembled that of Sarah Young, thus making nonsense of his plot if it were taken to represent her. He has accordingly given the woman a still attractive but more sophisticated appearance.

158. SCENE IN A GAMING HOUSE. Plate VI. Second state. Signed. 12⁷⁄₁₆ × 15¼ ins.

159. SCENE IN A GAMING HOUSE. Plate VI. Third state. Signed. 12⁷⁄₁₆ × 15¼ ins.

The Rake loses a second fortune by gambling, and frenziedly curses Heaven on his knees. A watchman and a fire break almost simultaneously into the room. Only the croupier and one of the gamblers have yet noticed it.

In the words of Paulson, 'The stages of the gambling madness can be traced across the print, from eagerness to passion to despair to apathy.'

The horseman seated before the fire is shown by the pistol and black mask in his pocket to be a highwayman. He, too, has lost his ill-gotten gains.

A fire broke out at White's on 3 May 1733, but the dog's collar bears the label 'Covent Garden'. He may belong to one of the gamblers or to the moneylender making out a receipt to Old Manners, brother to John Manners, Duke of Rutland, to whom the Duke of Devonshire lost the great estate of Leicester Abbey.

The changes in the third state are all technical, and include the correction of the shadow beneath the Rake's wig.

160. THE PRISON SCENE. Plate VII. Third state. Signed. 12½ × 15³⁄₁₆ ins.

161. THE PRISON SCENE. Plate VII. Fourth state. Signed. 12½ × 15³⁄₁₆ ins.

For the first time since he left his father's house the Rake is shown spending his time at home, the Fleet Prison for debtors. The serving boy and turnkey demand money, his wife upbraids him. Sarah Young, the heroine of the sub-plot, falls into convulsions as a result of witnessing his distress. She is horribly assisted by a debtor whose 'New Scheme for paying the Debts of the Nation' has dropped to the floor. The debtor at the back is a mad alchemist, among his crazy inventions is one for flying, but wings above the bed also refer to the fall of Icarus, who soared too near the sun.

Among the papers on the table beside the Rake is a manuscript returned by John Rich, manager of Covent Garden Theatre, with the laconic comment, 'I have read your Play and find it will not do.'

In the fourth state Hogarth has enhanced the macabre effect by dramatically darkening the plate with added hatching.

162. SCENE IN A MADHOUSE. Plate VIII. First state. $12\frac{7}{16} \times 15\frac{1}{4}$ ins. Royal Library, Windsor Castle.

163. SCENE IN A MADHOUSE. Plate VIII. Second state. $12\frac{7}{16} \times 15\frac{1}{4}$ ins.
The madhouse is Bedlam, for both the Rake and the fanatic who imagines himself a hermit in the cell behind him are modelled on two statues by Caius Gabriel Cibber, the sculptor father of the famous actor, on the gateway to the asylum.
Bedlam was a popular sight of London, being open to those members of the public who wished to combine charity with curiosity. Apart from the visitors and the two attendants, one of whom is fitting manacles to the Rake and the dog, all are lunatics, from left to right: a religious fanatic; a mad astronomer; behind him, a mad mathematician; a naked man who imagines himself a king; a gibbering tailor; a mad musician; a madman who imagines himself to be the Pope; and a melancholic who has been disappointed in love, for the name 'Charming Betty Careless' is carved on the stair rail in the second state. All have the consolations of a delusion, save the Rake and the lover. A patch shows that the Rake has attempted to stab himself, hence the manacles. Only one person sympathizes with his distress, Sarah Young, the humble girl he seduced while a student at Oxford and the heir to a great fortune.

164. THE SLEEPING CONGREGATION. December 1736. Etching and engraving. First state. Signed. $10 \times 7\frac{7}{8}$ ins. British Museum.
The text is 'Come unto me all ye that Labour and are Heavy Laden, and I shall give you Rest', *Matthew*, 11: 28. On the pulpit is inscribed 'I am afraid of you, lest I have bestowed upon you labour in vain', *Galatians*, 4: 11.
Only the preacher and the clerk are awake, the latter slyly observing the charms of a young girl who has fallen asleep while holding a prayer-book open at the service 'Of Matrimony'. The decorations are a satire on bad church art.

165–6. BEFORE AND AFTER. December 1736. Etching and engraving. Both signed.

165. BEFORE. First state. $14\frac{11}{16} \times 11\frac{15}{16}$ ins. Wilmarth S. Lewis collection.
The painting on the wall depicts Cupid lighting a rocket. The mobcap fastened to the curtain resembles the face of an onlooker.

166. AFTER. First state. $14\frac{9}{16} \times 12$ ins. Wilmarth S. Lewis collection.
A second painting has been added, showing Cupid laughing at the spent rocket. The dog is now asleep, beside a book of Aristotle open at the page '*Omne animal post coitum triste est*'.

167. SCHOLARS AT A LECTURE. January 1736/7. Etching and engraving. First state. Signed. $8\frac{3}{16} \times 6\frac{15}{16}$ ins. British Museum.
William Fisher of Jesus College, Oxford, Registrar of the University, agreed to be drawn for this satire on scholars at Oxford. His text commences 'Datur Vacuum', a pun on the two meanings of leisure and a vacuum.

168. THE COMPANY OF UNDERTAKERS. March 1736/7. Etching and engraving. Second state. Signed. $8\frac{5}{8} \times 7$ ins. British Museum.
The arms of the medical profession. Notice the urinal, the sable border decorated by cross-bones (the symbol of piracy and poison), the full-bottomed wigs and the gold-headed canes containing disinfectant in the heads, which some of the doctors smell. The text is a witty and elaborate parody on heraldic terminology. Hogarth originally intended to call the print *A Consultation of Quacks*, and there are 24 of these: twelve doctors and twelve gold-headed canes, the last being just as important and effective in the treatment of disease.
The likeness of famous doctors including Dr Joshua Ward, who treated Hogarth's friend Henry Fielding, is linked with that of notorious quacks like Mrs Sarah Mapp the bone-setter in the centre of the group at top. So far from annoying the medical profession, the print seems to have contributed to Hogarth's popularity with it.

169. THE DISTRESSED POET. March 1736/7. Etching and engraving. Second state. Signed. $12\frac{7}{16} \times 15\frac{5}{16}$ ins. British Museum.
The Grub Street poet, who is at a loss for ideas about his theme, 'Poverty', and the young devoted wife mending his one pair of breeches are interrupted by a milkmaid demanding payment. His dog steals a chop, placed with characteristic thoughtlessness on a low chair.
The print underwent curious changes. The picture over his head shows in the first state Alexander Pope as an ape, a pun on his signature A.P..e. In this state Pope is a hero, thrashing his antagonist Edmund Curll. Thereafter Hogarth never attacks Pope. Perhaps mutual friends brought about a reconciliation. In the third state the poet is writing a poem on Riches, and the print depicts 'A View of the Gold Mines of Peru'. The last change was probably made so that the print could be a companion picture to the *Enraged Musician* (No. 184) and a third satire which was projected on painting.

170–6. SEVEN ILLUSTRATIONS FOR CERVANTES 'DON QUIXOTE'. 1738. Etching and engraving. All signed, except the first. British Museum.

For a proposed Spanish edition under the patronage of Lord Carteret. Because his audience was to have been Spanish, Hogarth adopted an ambitious style partly based on Salvator Rosa. Perhaps fortunately, the project failed, and Hogarth became popular in Spain for his more original works.

170. THE FIRST SALLY IN QUEST OF ADVENTURE. Second state. Inscribed 'Vol. I, p. 7'. $9\frac{1}{16} \times 7\frac{1}{4}$ ins.

171. THE FUNERAL OF CHRYSOSTOM. First state. $9 \times 6\frac{15}{16}$ ins.

172. QUIXOTE CARED FOR BY THE INNKEEPER'S WIFE AND DAUGHTER. First state. $9 \times 6\frac{7}{8}$ ins.

173. THE ADVENTURE OF MAMBRINO'S HELMET. First state. $8\frac{7}{8} \times 7\frac{1}{16}$ ins.
Don Quixote attacks the barber.

174. THE FREEING OF THE GALLEY SLAVES. First state. $8\frac{13}{16} \times 7\frac{1}{8}$ ins.

175. DON QUIXOTE AND THE KNIGHT OF THE ROCK. First state. $9\frac{5}{16} \times 7\frac{1}{16}$ ins.

176. THE CURATE AND THE BARBER DISGUISING THEMSELVES. First state. $9 \times 6\frac{5}{8}$ ins.

177–80. THE FOUR TIMES OF THE DAY. May 1738. Etching and engraving. *Morning, Noon* and *Night* were executed by Hogarth, *Evening* by B. Baron after four paintings commissioned by Jonathan Tyers about 1736, for the decoration of Vauxhall Gardens, the fashionable pleasure gardens on the South Bank of the Thames. British Museum.

Because the pictures were painted for the private Vauxhall Gardens, then attracting the patronage of the aristocracy, they parody well-known public scenes of middle-class and vulgar entertainment in London.

177. MORNING. First state. $18\frac{1}{16} \times 14\frac{7}{8}$ ins.
Covent Garden in winter. On the right St Paul's Church by Inigo Jones. Tom King's Coffee House has been transferred from the other side of the square to fit it in the picture.

A spinster is on her way to church, attended by a foot-boy who carries her prayer-book. She is horrified to observe the conduct of two late revellers paying their attentions to young wenches of the market. As Paulson has pointed out, Hogarth here plays on the ideas of age and winter, youth and warmth. All the characters are warming themselves in different ways, only the elderly spinster is in accord with the bitter weather.

In the background two little boys are on their way to school, the quack Dr Rock advertises his panacea, and a fight has started in the coffee-house.

Thomas Fielding, Smollett and William Cowper all admired the marvellous image of the spinster, immortalized as Bridget Allworthy in the novel *Tom Jones*.

178. NOON. First state. $17\frac{3}{4} \times 15$ ins. The season is now spring and the scene is a street flanked by an eating-house and on one side a tavern and on the other a chapel, with the steeple of St Giles-in-the-Fields in the distance.

The chapel is being attended for Sunday morning service by Huguenot refugees, who have prospered in English trade and commerce. The old preserve the simplicity and customs of their ancestors; the young are dressed in the height of fashion; and the two male children are garbed like Judge and Milord respectively, an apt summary of the rise of the Huguenots in England.

By contrast, the English world on the left is extraordinarily careless. The boy carrying a dish from a baking-house has dropped and smashed it, and spilled the contents; the handsome young girl allows a Negro to take improper liberties with her person, and a quarrelling woman empties a shoulder of mutton, vegetables, etc., from a window. The crying boy (taken from Poussin's *Rape of the Sabines* now in the Metropolitan Museum, New York) does not even notice the ragged girl helping herself to the food which it is his duty to deliver.

179. EVENING. Second state. Engraved by B. Baron. $17\frac{7}{8} \times 14\frac{3}{4}$ ins.
Summer at Sadler's Wells, the bourgeois counterpart to the aristocratic Vauxhall.

A citizen, his wife and family promenade outside the Sadler's Wells Theatre and the Sir Hugh Middleton Tavern, named after the philanthropist who brought water from the north into London by conduits (see the foreground) leading out of the Islington reservoir.

In this print, woman is presented as a vexation and not a blessing to man. The masterful, sensual and pregnant wife has cuckolded her docile husband, hence the cow who supplies the horns. The daughter scolds her younger brother who has been given his father's walking stick as a hobby-horse, and points accusingly at the gingerbread cake in the shape of a king.

180. NIGHT. First state. $17\frac{5}{16} \times 14\frac{1}{2}$ ins.

The scene is a street leading to Charing Cross, dominated by the statue of Charles I by Le Sueur. Bagnios are advertised on both sides. A fire in the middle of the street has alarmed the horse, and the passenger coach is overturned. In the centre a freemason in full regalia (alleged to be Sir Thomas De Veil, a Bow Street magistrate notorious for the severity of his punishments and the laxity of his private life) reels home drunk after attending a masonic lodge.

The barber's signpost advertises dentistry. The oakleaves celebrate the 29th of May, anniversary of the restoration (1660) of Charles II, patron of brothels.

181. STROLLING ACTRESSES DRESSING IN A BARN. May 1738. Etching and engraving. Second state. Signed. $16\frac{3}{4} \times 21\frac{1}{4}$ ins. British Museum.

'For wit and imagination', wrote Horace Walpole, 'without any other end . . . the best of all his works.'

On 27 June 1737, the *Act Against Strolling Players* (on the crown left foreground) made it an offence to perform plays without a licence outside the City of London and Westminster. This country company evades the law by presenting a play with a cast of women and children, for the Act specifies actors, not actresses. The playbill on the bed reveals that they are going to perform *The Devil to Pay in Heaven* and that the *dramatis personae* are Juno, Diana, Flora, Night, a Siren, Aurora, an Eagle, Cupid, two Devils and Ghost and Attendants. To the left of Diana stands an altar, beside which two little devils are quarrelling over a tankard of porter. On the top of the altar is a burning pipe without a lid. The threatened blow with the fist will scatter its fire. A candle is already setting light to the basket in which the company's stage jewellery is kept. The whole barn will shortly go up in flames, and there will be the devil to pay in this mock Council of the Gods.

Cupid climbs a ladder to get a pair of stockings for Apollo. On the left Ganymede (without breeches) suffers from toothache and is offered a drink of gin by the Siren. Flora dresses her hair with a candle. Diana in the centre declaims her lines. A page and the Ghost operate on a cat to obtain blood for the ghost scene. Night darns a hole in Juno's stocking, while a monkey makes water into the helmet of Jupiter. The two devils are a parody of the children in Raphael's *The Sacrifice at Lystra*.

An unobserved youth looks at the proceedings through a hole in the roof.

182. THE FOUNDLING HOSPITAL POWER OF ATTORNEY. 1739. Third state. Engraved by La Cave after Hogarth's design. Headpiece. $4\frac{1}{2} \times 8\frac{1}{4}$ ins.

The power of attorney authorized the Hospital to collect subscriptions. The central figure beside the beadle is Captain Thomas Coram, the founder of the Hospital, holding its Royal Charter.

183. HYMEN AND CUPID. August 1740. $5\frac{7}{8} \times 7\frac{7}{16}$ ins. British Museum.

A ticket for the masque *Alfred the Great, King of England*, by David Mallet and James Thomson, for which the musician Dr Thomas Arne composed *Rule, Britannia*. It was performed at Cliveden in Buckinghamshire (shown in the background), at that time the country house of Frederick, Prince of Wales.

184. THE ENRAGED MUSICIAN. November 1741. Etching and engraving. Second state. Signed. $13\frac{1}{16} \times 15\frac{11}{16}$ ins. British Museum.

The musician at the window is driven nearly mad by the noises emanating from the following, in order from left to right: a ballad singer, a screeching parrot, a girl with a rattle, an itinerant hautboy player, a milk-girl calling her wares, a boy drummer, a barking dog, a paviour, a dustman, a knife-grinder, a sow-gelder blowing his horn and a bawling fish-pedlar. In the background cats fight noisily on the roof of a pewterer's shop.

185. THE CHARMERS OF THE AGE. 1741. Etching by R. Livesay after Hogarth's drawing, and published posthumously by Mrs Hogarth in 1782. $6\frac{5}{8} \times 9\frac{11}{16}$ ins. W. S. Lewis collection.

A satire on the opera dancers Desnoyer and La Barbarina.

186. MARTIN FOLKES. 1742. Etching and engraving. Fourth state. Signed. $11 \times 8\frac{15}{16}$ ins. British Museum.

Martin Folkes was President of the Royal Society.

187. THE DISCOVERY. *c.* 1743. Etching. Proof before lettering. $6\frac{1}{4} \times 7\frac{5}{16}$ ins. British Museum.

A practical joke on the actor-manager John Highmore. The composition is borrowed from the illustration by Lancret to *Le Gascon puni* by La Fontaine.

188. CHARACTERS AND CARICATURAS. April 1743. Etching. First state. Signed. $7\frac{11}{16} \times 8\frac{1}{8}$ ins. British Museum.

The subscription ticket to *Marriage-à-la-Mode*, and like *Boys peeping at Nature* an important manifesto of his aims. Hogarth declares that he is not a caricaturist, but a comic history painter. The mirror that he holds up to Nature is a truthful one, and does not distort, like the enormities of the caricaturist.

189. BISHOP HOADLY. July 1743. Etching and engraving by Bernard Baron. Signed. $13\frac{15}{16} \times 11\frac{1}{4}$ ins. British Museum.
Benjamin Hoadly, Bishop of Winchester, was a close friend of Hogarth, and shared his liberal and humanitarian ideals. A Whig in favour with the government, he wears the Order of the Garter.

190. THE BATTLE OF THE PICTURES. February 1744/5. Etching. $7 \times 7\frac{7}{8}$ ins. British Museum.
A ticket for the auction of nineteen paintings by Hogarth, including *The Harlot's Progress* and *The Rake's Progress*. The idea is taken from Swift.
In front of the auction rooms of Mr Cock (see the weather-vane), an army of Old Master paintings, headed by *Apollo flaying Marsyas*, *Europa and the Bull*, *St Francis* piercing the prude in *Morning*, *Mary Magdalen* invading the Harlot's bedchamber and the *Aldobrandini Wedding* denting *Marriage-à-la-Mode*, is moving to the assault of Hogarth's studio, where his auction was to be held.
In the air, however, the *Feast of Olympus* and the *Procession of Bacchus* fail to make a hole in the Tavern Scene from *The Rake's Progress* and the *Midnight Modern Conversation*.
The pictures labelled D and Ditto are copies and fakes.

191. MASK AND PALETTE. 1745. Etching. $4 \times 4\frac{1}{2}$ ins. British Museum.
Subscription ticket for Garrick as *Richard III*.

192. HEADPIECE FOR THE LONDON INFIRMARY. 1745. Etching and engraving by Charles Grignion. Signed. $6\frac{1}{2} \times 9$ ins. British Museum.
For a brochure on the Hospital founded in 1740. Christ points to an ancient hospital and exhorts His Disciples, including Judas in shadow.

193-8. MARRIAGE-À-LA-MODE. June 1745. 6 plates. Etching and engraving. British Museum. The prints are reproduced opposite the original paintings in the Tate Gallery, London. These are all 27×35 ins. and were begun just before Hogarth's visit to Paris in 1743. The French influence is so strong that he probably made a fresh start after his return.

193.*THE MARRIAGE CONTRACT. Oil on canvas.

193. THE MARRIAGE CONTRACT. Plate I. Fourth state. Engraved by G. Scotin. Signed. $14 \times 17\frac{1}{2}$ ins.
The Earl of Squanderfield and a rich Alderman of the City of London arrange a marriage between son and daughter respectively, the former to pay off a mortgage on his estate and also to finish building a magnificent Palladian mansion, the latter to ennoble his descendants. At the window the merchant's lawyer, used to the City, marvels at the extravagant new mansion. Before him a moneylender returns the redeemed mortgage. Counsellor Silvertongue, the fashionable lawyer employed by the Earl, takes advantage of the boredom of the bride playing absentmindedly with her ring, and pays adroit court to her, while the bridegroom Viscount Squanderfield, turns his back in the direction of a mirror. In front of him two dogs are chained together against their will, an indication of the future state of the young couple.
The Earl points to his family tree showing his descent from William, Duke of Normandy. His coronet, the symbol of his pride, is everywhere, above the canopy, on his footstool and crutch, and absurdly on the flank of the couchant dog. The pictures on the wall are all Dark Masters: their theme is catastrophe or martyrdom. David prepares to cut off Goliath's head; Judith has already removed that of Holofernes; St Sebastian is pierced by arrows; St Laurence is being grilled; Prometheus is torn by the vulture; and the Innocents are massacred. Most are copies after Titian, as is also the *Destruction of Pharaoh's Host*, on the ceiling. The portrait of the Earl as a hero of Marlborough's campaign is a parody of Le Brun, and is rendered sublime by a comet, a thunderbolt and a cannon exploding too close for his comfort or safety. Already his robes and wig fly in opposite directions.

194.*THE BREAKFAST SCENE. Oil on canvas.

194. THE BREAKFAST SCENE. Plate II. Second state. Engraved by B. Baron. $14 \times 17\frac{5}{8}$ ins.
The Lady Squanderfield is taking morning tea at 1:20 p.m. after giving a card and music party which has lasted through the night. Her husband has just returned from an excursion of dissipation, for his dog is smelling the handkerchief of a strange woman which hangs out of his pocket. The Methodist steward, a pamphlet entitled *Regeneration* in his pocket, holds up his hand in horror as he walks out with a thick pile of bills and only one receipt. The interior ridicules the style of William Kent in interior decoration, the rococo, and the cult of Old Masters and the antique. St Matthew, St John the Baptist and St Andrew flank a nude, covered by a curtain except for one of her feet. The classical bust has an authentic crack on the nose, and is surrounded by Chinese and Indian curiosities. On the rococo clock a cat hungrily eyes two large fish swimming inappropriately among foliage.

195.*THE SCENE WITH THE QUACK. Oil on canvas.

195. THE SCENE WITH THE QUACK. Plate III. First state. Engraved by B. Baron. 13⅞ × 17¹¹⁄₁₆ ins.

The Viscount brings two women to a quack doctor to discover which has infected him. The young girl in tears is a servant whom he has seduced. The older woman is a prostitute, who draws her clasp-knife and threatens violence to prevent being examined. The quack, who wipes his spectacles for the examination, is hardened to taunts about the uselessness of his pills which the Viscount has taken as a precaution. Instead of being frightened, he appears highly amused. The expression of the Rake is modelled on one of Le Brun's *Passions*, 'Acute Pain'.

The room is the 'museum' of Dr Misaubin, 96 St Martin's Lane, Westminster. His collection of instruments and curiosities can be seen: two machines, one for straightening a dislocated limb, the other for drawing a cork from a bottle; a crocodile with an ostrich's egg hanging from its belly; the head of a monstrous child; a narwhal's tusk; and the paraphernalia of his profession. In the cupboard, surmounted by a tripod in the shape of the triple gallows at Tyburn, a life-size anatomical figure receives the lecherous advances of a skeleton. On the other side the doctor's wig is set on a block which is also the effigy of an identified rake.

196.*THE COUNTESS'S LEVEE. Oil on canvas.

196. THE COUNTESS'S LEVEE. Plate IV. Second state. Engraved by S. Ravenet. 13⅞ × 17⅝ ins.

The Countess, whose bed is now crowned by an Earl's coronet, showing that her father-in-law has died, is having her hair dressed by a French hairdresser, while she receives a somewhat mixed company. On the sofa Counsellor Silvertongue points to a masquerade scene on the screen with one hand and holds out invitingly a ticket with the other. The male singer is probably the castrato mezzo-soprano Francesco Bernardi, called Senesino, accompanied by the German flautist Weidemann. The audience of amateurs reacts in different ways to the performance. The dandy in hair-curlers, identified as Herr Michel, the Prussian envoy, sips chocolate. The gentleman with the fan affects to be entranced. The country squire with a riding whip is fast asleep. The lady in raptures has been identified as Mrs Fox Lane, Lady Bingley, who once exclaimed 'One God, one Farinelli'. The miscellaneous *objets d'art* on the floor have been bought at the auction of the Late Sir Timothy Babyhouse, and reflect his infantile taste. Cards on the floor invite 'Lady Squanders' to routs at the home of Lady Hairbrain, Lady Heathen, etc. On the sofa is a copy of the erotic poem *Le Sopha* by Crébillon fils, and the same theme is repeated by the Old Masters: *Lot tempted to drink by his Daughters*, Correggio's *Jupiter and Io*, and Correggio's *Rape of Ganymede*. The portrait of Counsellor Silvertongue marks the extent of her infatuation, which is obvious even to her Negro page who is pointing to Actaeon's horns.

197.*THE DEATH OF THE EARL. Oil on canvas.

197. THE DEATH OF THE EARL. Plate V. Third state. Engraved by S. Ravenet. 13¹⁵⁄₁₆ × 17⅝ ins.

The young Earl of Squanderfield, belatedly conscious of his honour, has followed his wife to the Turk's Head bagnio, or brothel, where she has an assignation, in a private chamber, with Counsellor Silvertongue. They fight, the earl is mortally wounded and dies in an exquisite parody of the serpentine line of grace. The watch break in at the door, while the Counsellor prudently retires out of the window. The picture over the door is St Luke with his ox, and takes hints for an Old Master painting in the grand manner. The tapestry depicts the *Judgment of Solomon*, for the Countess has chosen between husband and lover, and will shortly lose both. The portrait of a prostitute is hung over legs in the akimbo stance of Henry VIII. In the painting the light of the fire is marvellously handled.

Counsellor Silvertongue had taken his position for the duel so that the light shone in his adversary's eyes.

198.*THE DEATH OF THE COUNTESS. Oil on canvas.

198. THE DEATH OF THE COUNTESS. Plate VI. Second state. Engraved by G. Scotin. 13¹⁵⁄₁₆ × 17⁹⁄₁₆ ins.

The scene is the home of the Alderman by Old London Bridge. On the floor lies a broadsheet, *Counsellor Silvertongue's last Dying Speech*, for the commoner who killed an Earl in a duel has been hanged at Tyburn. Overwhelmed with grief, the Countess has bribed a servant (left) with the gift of one of her father's coats to procure laudanum, which she has swallowed. The apothecary, who has been summoned too late, upbraids the innocently stupid servant. The merchant callously removes her valuable ring, the one item of profit in the whole transaction, before she is dead. Only her old nurse and the child show grief or affection.

The child is a girl and has rickets. The posterity of the proud old Earl has been disgraced and by the law of male descent the merchant's family will not inherit the title.

The appearance of the room ridicules the meanness of the merchant and his taste in art. Like the aristocrat, he admires only what is foreign, in this case not high Italian but low Dutch art. An emaciated dog with suspicious eyes is hoping to carry off a pig's head before normal life is restored.

199. GARRICK IN THE CHARACTER OF RICHARD III. July 1746. Second state. Etching and engraving by Hogarth and C. Grignion. 15¼ × 19¹⁵⁄₁₆ ins. British Museum.

The friend of Hogarth in the Shakespearean rôle by which he first became famous. Richard awakens from his nightmare in Act V, Scene 8. Influenced by Le Brun's *The Family of Darius before Alexander*.

200. TASTE IN HIGH LIFE. May 1746. Etching. Engraver unknown. First state. $7\frac{3}{4} \times 10\frac{3}{8}$ ins. British Museum.
Said to have been engraved against Hogarth's wishes by an unknown hand.
The picture was painted in 1742 for Miss Mary Edwards of Kensington who wished to retaliate against people who made fun of her old-fashioned clothes. The satire is directed against the Frenchified tastes of high society. The beau is believed to be the second Earl of Portmore, who had spent some years at the French court, and the blackamoor page is Ignatius Sancho, later painted by Gainsborough. On the floor are cards, a pyramid of dominoes and a monkey reading a French menu headed 'Pour Dinner'. The courses are coxcombs, ducks' tongues, rabbits' ears, fricassée of snails and 'grande d'Oeufs Beurre'. The pictures on the wall depict the French dancing master Desnoyer among other nasty insects, the Venus de Medici on high heels, with her hoop-petticoat cut away to reveal the contrast with the actual figure, Cupid tending to a fire made up of articles of costume which deform beauty, and a lady walking with as much difficulty as the blind man on the far side of the wall. The woman in the sedan chair has had to lift up her hoop in order to get inside.

201. SIMON LORD LOVAT. August 1746. Etching in aquafortis. Second state. Signed. $13\frac{3}{16} \times 8\frac{7}{8}$ ins. British Museum.
Hogarth drew Simon Fraser, Lord Lovat, at St Albans on his way to London to be executed for his part in the Jacobite rebellion of 1745. The Highland chief is shown counting the clans that fought for the Pretender.

202. A COUNTRY INN YARD AT ELECTION TIME. June 1747. Etching and engraving. Second state. Signed. $8\frac{1}{8} \times 11\frac{7}{8}$ ins. British Museum.
A satire on the candidature of John Tylney, Viscount Castlemaine, as Member of Parliament for Essex at the age of twenty — hence the baby being carried in procession by his opponents.
The election agent in the foreground has a copy of the Act against bribery in his pocket. Nevertheless, he is reluctantly prepared to pay the exorbitant bill presented by the innkeeper, as a secret bribe for his support.
On the roof of the coach a sailor from Lord Anson's ship *Centurion*, which began the battle against the French fleet off Cape Finisterre on 9 April 1747, slyly prepares to knock off the hat of the Frenchman who is dejected by the news of the English victory.

203–14. INDUSTRY AND IDLENESS. October 1747. 12 plates. Etching with some engraving, and engraved frames. Signed. British Museum.
Hogarth himself stated that he adopted a simple style and sold the prints at a shilling each in order to reach those for whom his moral message was intended.

203.*THE FELLOW 'PRENTICES AT THEIR LOOMS. Pen and brown ink, and grey washes over pencil. $10\frac{3}{8} \times 13$ ins. British Museum.

203. THE FELLOW 'PRENTICES AT THEIR LOOMS. Plate I. Second state. $10\frac{3}{16} \times 13\frac{3}{8}$ ins.
'The Drunkard shall come to Poverty, and drowsiness shall cloath a Man with rags.' *Proverbs*, 23:21. Under Thomas Idle.
'The hand of the diligent maketh rich.' *Proverbs*, 10: 4. Under Frank (Francis) Goodchild.
The scene is a silk-weaving manufacture at Spitalfields, belonging to Mr West. Above Idle's head, a copy of *Moll Flanders*, the story of a fallen woman by Daniel Defoe. Below Goodchild a well-kept copy of the *Prentices Guide*.

204. THE INDUSTRIOUS 'PRENTICE PERFORMING THE DUTY OF A CHRISTIAN. Plate II. First state. $10\frac{3}{16} \times 13\frac{7}{16}$ ins.
'O! How I love thy Law it is my meditation all the day.' *Psalms*, 119: 97.
The congregation is divided into those who sing, stare and sleep. The pew-opener faces the entrance to prevent late arrivals from interrupting the singing of the psalm. Frank Goodchild shares his book with the daughter of his master.

205. THE IDLE 'PRENTICE AT PLAY IN THE CHURCH YARD, DURING DIVINE SERVICE. Plate III. First state. $10\frac{1}{8} \times 13\frac{7}{8}$ ins.
'Judgments are prepar'd for Scorners, and Stripes for the back of Fools.' *Proverbs*, 19: 29.
Tom Idle, on a tombstone beside a grave that has just been dug, is detected cheating a shoe-black. The grave is the postponed judgment, the cane of the parish beadle will immediately deliver the stripes.

206. THE INDUSTRIOUS 'PRENTICE A FAVOURITE, AND ENTRUSTED BY HIS MASTER. Plate IV. First state. $9\frac{15}{16} \times 13\frac{5}{16}$ ins.
'Well done thou good and faithfull Servant thou hast been faithfull over a few things, I will make thee Ruler over many things.' *Matthew*, 25: 21.

The clasped gloves on the desk symbolize the relationship between Goodchild and his master, West. On the *London Almanac* Industry seizes Time by the forelock. The dress of Goodchild, his keys, purse and ledger indicate a position of trust and responsibility.

207. THE IDLE 'PRENTICE TURN'D AWAY, AND SENT TO SEA. Plate V. Second state. 10 × 13 5/16 ins.
'A Foolish Son is the heaviness of his Mother.' *Proverbs*, 10: 1.
Dismissed by his master (the forfeited indentures of apprenticeship have been dropped into the water), Tom Idle has been sent to sea, to the grief of his widowed mother. He is taunted by a boy dangling a cat-o'-nine-tails and a waterman pointing to the gibbet at Cuckolds Point on the Thames, but retaliates by making the sign of two horns with his fingers.

208.*THE INDUSTRIOUS 'PRENTICE OUT OF HIS TIME, AND MARRIED TO HIS MASTER'S DAUGHTER. Plate VI. Pencil and pen with black ink on white paper. 8 1/4 × 11 5/8 ins. In the collection of Mr and Mrs Paul Mellon.

208. THE INDUSTRIOUS 'PRENTICE OUT OF HIS TIME, AND MARRIED TO HIS MASTER'S DAUGHTER. Plate VI. Second state. 10 × 13 1/4 ins.
The sign shows that Goodchild and West are now partners and live in a handsome house near the Monument. The wedding celebrations are attended by a band of drummers, musicians, two butchers with bones and cleavers and a well-known personality at City weddings, Philip in the Tub, singing a new song, 'Jesse, or the Happy Pair'. The allusion is to the Tree of Jesse. The footman makes the traditional gift of the remains of the banquet to a poor woman.

209. THE IDLE 'PRENTICE RETURN'D FROM SEA, AND IN A GARRET WITH A COMMON PROSTITUTE. Plate VII. First state. 10 1/8 × 13 7/16 ins.
'The Sound of a Shaken Leaf should Chase him.' *Leviticus*, 26: 36.
Tom Idle, now a highway thief, has also found a partner to share his common life. The prostitute admires his loot and holds up an ear-ring in the shape of a gallows, while he is terrified by the noise made by a cat falling down the chimney after a rat. The door is barricaded against the officers of the law.

210. THE INDUSTRIOUS 'PRENTICE GROWN RICH, AND SHERIFF OF LONDON. Plate VIII. First state. 10 × 13 5/16 ins.
'With all thy getting get understanding. Exalt her, and she shall promote thee: she shall bring thee to honour, when thou dost Embrace her.' *Proverbs*, 4: 7, 8.
Goodchild and his wife preside over a civic banquet under the portrait of William III. The beadle in the foreground pompously receives a petition addressed to the new Sheriff.
The group of diners on the left constitute a satire on gluttony.

211. THE IDLE 'PRENTICE BETRAY'D BY HIS WHORE, AND TAKEN IN A NIGHT CELLAR WITH HIS ACCOMPLICE. Plate IX. Second state. 10 1/4 × 13 5/16 ins.
'The Adulteress shall hunt for the precious life.' *Proverbs*, 6: 26.
The scene is the cellar of the Blood Bowl House, Blood Bowl Alley. While Idle and his accomplice quarrel over their share of the spoils, the prostitute betrays him to a magistrate for money. The magistrate will have an opportunity for more than one arrest. A brawl has broken out, and the corpse of a murdered man is being thrown through a trap-door.

212. THE INDUSTRIOUS 'PRENTICE ALDERMAN OF LONDON, THE IDLE ONE BROUGHT BEFORE HIM AND IMPEACHED BY HIS ACCOMPLICE. Plate X. First state. 10 × 13 1/4 ins.
'The Wicked is snar'd in the work of his own hands.' *Psalms*, 9: 16. Under Thomas Idle.
'Thou shalt do no unrighteousness in Judgment.' *Leviticus*, 19: 15. Under Frank Goodchild.
In a Court of Justice the Alderman in his rôle of magistrate is forced to commit Idle to Newgate. The superstitious accomplice who is his second betrayer swears with his left hand while a wench bribes the attendant not to notice that he is doing so. His weeping mother intercedes in vain with the beadle.

213. THE IDLE 'PRENTICE EXECUTED AT TYBURN. Plate XI. Second state. 10 1/8 × 15 3/4 ins.
'When fear cometh as desolation, and their destruction cometh as a whirlwind; when distress cometh upon them, then they shall call upon God, but he will not answer.' *Proverbs*, 1: 27, 28.
A pigeon, released from the grandstand, carries the news that Idle is approaching the gallows. A Methodist preacher accompanies him in the cart, and has converted him to piety and repentance. The officiating clergyman of the Church of England rides ahead in state.
In the cart on the extreme right, Idle's mother hides her face in horror and despair. Drinking gin in the next cart is Mother Douglas, a well-known bawd, who has decided to give the ladies of her establishment an edifying treat.

In the crowd pickpockets, vendors, brawlers, soldiers, boys and beggars are variously occupied, and a ruffian prepares to hurl a dog at the Methodist preacher. In the centre a woman with a child is selling a broadsheet, *The last Dying Speech and Confession of Tho. Idle*, written fictitiously and printed by a speculator before the event.

For the first time the borders are changed. Hitherto the emblems have been a cat-o'-nine-tails, manacles and a hangman's rope for Tom Idle, and the mace of the City of London, an alderman's gold chain and a sword of state for Frank Goodchild. Here human skeletons hang by staples passed through their crania.

214. THE INDUSTRIOUS 'PRENTICE LORD MAYOR OF LONDON. Plate XII. Second state. $10\frac{15}{16} \times 15\frac{3}{4}$ ins.
'Length of days is in her right hand, and in her left hand Riches and Honour.' *Proverbs*, 3 : 16. The framing emblems are now the cornucopia of plenty.

Frank Goodchild is now Lord Mayor of London and rides in procession on Lord Mayor's Day, the 5th of November. To complete his success, he is being watched by Frederick Prince of Wales and his consort from a balcony.

An emaciated boy sells a broadsheet entitled *A Full and true Account of the Ghost of Tho. Idle*, who has become a legend and may well be remembered when Frank Goodchild is forgotten.

215. JACOBUS GIBBS. 1747. Etching and engraving by B. Baron after Hogarth. Third state. Signed. $10\frac{3}{16} \times 7\frac{3}{16}$ ins.
James Gibbs, the architect of St Martin-in-the-Fields, St Mary-le-Strand and the Senate House, Cambridge, had just completed his masterpiece, the Radcliffe Camera at Oxford, begun in 1737.

216. HEADPIECE TO 'THE JACOBITE'S JOURNAL'. December 1747. Woodcut. Engraver unknown. $4\frac{3}{8} \times 7\frac{1}{4}$ ins. In the collection of Wilmarth S. Lewis.
Hogarth's friend Henry Fielding published the first number of the Journal on 5 December 1747. Pretending to be a Jacobite writing for Jacobites, he attacked both Jacobites and those whom we today would call fellow-travellers.

A Scotsman and his wife ride an ass led by a friar with a finger to the side of his nose. Three fleurs-de-lis decorate the *Commonwealth of Oceana* (1656) by James Harrington, who attended Charles I on the scaffold, although a Republican by conviction.

216.*HEADPIECE TO 'THE JACOBITE'S JOURNAL'. 1747. Drawing for the above. Red chalk on paper. $8\frac{1}{4} \times 6\frac{3}{4}$ ins. Royal Library, Windsor Castle.

217. O THE ROAST BEEF OF OLD ENGLAND, OR THE GATE OF CALAIS. March 1748/9. Etching and engraving by Hogarth and C. Mosley after Hogarth's painting. Second state. Signed. $13\frac{5}{8} \times 17\frac{5}{16}$ ins. Royal Library, Windsor Castle.
On his way back from his second visit to Paris in 1748 Hogarth was arrested as a spy at Calais for sketching the English arms on one of the old gates, inside the modern fortifications. This was his retaliation, based on a song by Henry Fielding, contrasting English beef with French syllabubs.

A cook staggers with a huge sirloin of beef, which he is delivering from the ship to Madam Grandsire's, the English eating-house in Calais. The phenomenon is closely inspected by the greedy friar, openly admired by the two ragged French soldiers and covertly glanced at by the Irish soldier taking his stew. The Scottish soldier sitting beside his barley-cake and onion is brooding over the failure of the 1745 Rebellion. A group of grinning fisherwomen are amused to detect the resemblance to a human face in a huge skate, without realizing that their own faces are just as much a caricature of nature. Through the arch, priests are seen on their way to administer extreme unction under the tavern sign of the Dove or Holy Spirit.

Hogarth has introduced his own portrait beside the sentry box on the left. His attention appears to be divided between the episode of the sirloin and the old gate, which bears a ludicrous resemblance to a gaping mouth: the spikes are like teeth, the shields serve for eyes (Paulson). The hand of the soldier making the arrest is seen on the artist's back.

218. GUGLIELMUS HOGARTH. 1748/9. Etching and engraving. Fourth state. Signed. $13\frac{1}{2} \times 10\frac{5}{16}$ ins. British Museum.
This is the famous manifesto portrait, showing the Line of Beauty on his palette, the works of Shakespeare, Milton and Swift and his pug dog Trump.

219. A STAND OF ARMS, MUSICAL INSTRUMENTS, ETC. March 1749/50. Etching and engraving. $6\frac{3}{4} \times 8$ ins. British Museum.
The subscription ticket for the *March to Finchly*. The musical instruments, bagpipes, trumpet, etc., are also connected with war. A pair of scissors invades the scroll and is cutting out the Lion of Scotland from the shield of arms.

220. VIEW OF RANBY'S HOUSE, CHISWICK, FROM HOGARTH'S VILLA. 1750. Etching, published by Jane Hogarth in 1781. Second state. $3\frac{3}{16} \times 5\frac{7}{8}$ ins. British Museum.
Hogarth's neighbour and friend across the fields was principal sergeant-surgeon to George II.

221-2. BEER STREET AND GIN LANE. February 1750/1. Etching and engraving. Both are signed.
These were political prints supporting a ministerial measure against the unlimited sale of gin. The Gin Act was passed

in the summer after the prints appeared. Verses were written by Hogarth's friend and collaborator, the dramatist the Rev. James Townley.

221. BEER STREET. Second state. $14\frac{1}{8} \times 11\frac{15}{16}$ ins. British Museum.

A scene of London life and industry in which tradesmen, craftsmen and labourers thrive on the national beverage, beer. In consequence, the shop of the pawnbroker N. Pinch is crumbling in ruins.

A jolly butcher laughs at a cooper manhandling a Frenchman. Beneath the sign of the *Barley Mow* a ragged French signpainter adds a second sign advertising gin, with the consequences shown in the next plate.

The waste books in the basket being carried to a trunk-maker are all by authors whom Hogarth disliked: Dr John Hill's criticism of the Royal Society, George Turnbull's eulogy of ancient painting and William Lauder's attack on his hero Milton.

In the third state Hogarth removed the Frenchman with his portmanteau and substituted an English courting couple. But the hostility to France, to whose art he owed so much, had to remain in an age in which the two great countries were imperial rivals.

222.*GIN LANE. Drawing for the engraving. Red chalk with pencil additions. $16\frac{1}{2} \times 12$ ins. Pierpont Morgan Library.

222. GIN LANE. Second state. $14\frac{3}{16} \times 12$ ins. British Museum.

The shop of the pawnbroker S. Gripe is now flourishing, as is the gin cellar below and the distillery at the right. Suicide, murder, starvation, disease and destitution afflict the working people, and children are the worst victims. The man who has hanged himself is a barber, since no one can afford his services. The steeple of St George's, Bloomsbury, is seen in the distance.

223. THE MARCH TO FINCHLY. December 1750. Eighth state. Etching and engraving by Luke Sullivan. Retouched and improved by Hogarth, 12 June 1761. $16\frac{5}{16} \times 21\frac{1}{2}$ ins. British Museum.

Published five years after the Rebellion of 1745, the satire may be linked with an attempt to introduce stricter discipline in the army, on the model of the army of Frederick II of Prussia, to whom the third and subsequent states were dedicated.

Outside the King's Head Tavern with its signpost of Charles II, the patron of bordellos, at Tottenham Court Road Turnpike, the English foot guards are saying farewell before marching against the Pretender. The bawd Mother Douglas prays for their safety at a window, and the ladies of her establishment are affected in a variety of ways. The episodes are similar to those in the execution scene of *The Idle 'Prentice* (No. 213). The central group is a parody of *Hercules between Vice and Virtue* by Rubens in the Uffizi Gallery. Both the young ballad-singer on the left and the older newsvendor on the right are pregnant. The former is selling a portrait of the military hero the Duke of Cumberland, and a copy of *God Save our Noble King*. The latter is a Papist, selling copies of *The Jacobite Journal*. The first has yielded to the soldier, he has yielded to the latter. His choice is between youth, honour and patriotism, and domination by a Roman Catholic virago. This symbolizes the political choice of the country.

George II, who was proud of the Guards, is said to have refused the original dedication.

224–7. THE FOUR STAGES OF CRUELTY. February 1750/1. Etching and some engraving. All signed. British Museum.

The verses are probably by the Rev. James Townley.

224.*THE FIRST STAGE OF CRUELTY. Drawing for the engraving. Pencil over rough red chalk on white paper. Incised, and the back reddened. $14\frac{3}{8} \times 11\frac{3}{4}$ ins. on a sheet $15\frac{3}{4} \times 11\frac{3}{4}$ ins. In the collection of Mr and Mrs Paul Mellon.

224. THE FIRST STAGE OF CRUELTY. First state. $14 \times 11\frac{11}{16}$ ins.

The central figure is Tom Nero, wearing the badge of the Parish of St Giles, and his destiny is predicted by the drawing on the wall. An extraordinary detail is the cat, fitted with wings, being thrown from a dormer window.

The boy rushing to intercede with a tart in his hand is said to be a compliment to the future George III, then aged thirteen, whose father Frederick, Prince of Wales, died later in the same year. Like many liberals, Hogarth favoured the court party of Frederick, who was an enlightened and *avant-garde* patron of the arts.

225. THE SECOND STAGE OF CRUELTY. First state. $13\frac{7}{8} \times 11\frac{15}{16}$ ins.

The scene is a street at the entrance of Thavies Inn and Coffee-house. The placards advertise prizefighting and cockfighting. Once again Hogarth has simplified his style and avoided subtleties, so that his meaning is perfectly clear without a commentary.

226. CRUELTY IN PERFECTION. First state. $14 \times 11\frac{3}{4}$ ins.

Tom Nero is being arrested for the murder of his mistress, who has brought him valuables stolen from her employer. Two books have fallen out of the box, *God's Revenge against Murder* and *Common Prayer*.

The pathetic letter reads:

'Dear Tommy My Mistress has been the best of Women to me, and my Conscience flies in my face as often as I think of wronging her, yet I am resolved to venture Body and Soul to do as you would have me so don't fail to meet me as you said you would. For I shall bring along with me all the things I can lay my hands on. So no more at present but I remain yours till Death, Ann Gull.'

227. THE REWARD OF CRUELTY. Third state. $14 \times 11\frac{3}{4}$ ins.

Here is the Anatomy Lesson of the President of the Royal College of Physicians, seated beneath the device of the College, a hand feeling a pulse, and the Royal Arms. The skeletons are those of the pugilist James Field and the highwayman Macleane.

The noose has not been removed from Tom Nero's neck. His heart is about to be eaten by a dog.

228. PAUL BEFORE FELIX BURLESQUED. May 1751. Engraving with some mezzotint, and staining. First state. Signed. $9\frac{7}{8} \times 13\frac{1}{2}$ ins. British Museum.

The subscription ticket for *Paul before Felix* and *Moses Brought to Pharaoh's Daughter*.

A parody of the Dutch School, with a sly attack on Caravaggio (the bloated feet of the Angel). Paul is so short that he has to stand on a stool, Justice is fat and coarse, Felix trembles with fear and the prosecutor Tertullus tears up his speech in despair.

The publication line reads 'Design'd and scratch'd in the true Dutch taste'. Paulson has suggested that early impressions were stained with coffee.

229. PAUL BEFORE FELIX. February 1752. Etching and engraving. First state. Signed. $15\frac{1}{8} \times 20\frac{1}{16}$ ins. British Museum.

Felix sits on his throne of justice in the courtroom between his wife Drusilla and the High Priest Ananias. The text is from *Acts*, 24: 25: 'And as he reasoned of righteousness, temperance and judgment to come, Felix trembled.'

The style is strongly influenced by Rembrandt as well as Raphael, and shows that Hogarth was not opposed to the great Dutch master, only his lesser imitators. The original painting was commissioned for Lincoln's Inn, London, where it now hangs.

230. MOSES BROUGHT TO PHARAOH'S DAUGHTER. February 1752. Etching and engraving. Second state. Signed. $15\frac{5}{16} \times 19\frac{7}{8}$ ins. British Museum.

The original picture was painted for the Foundling Hospital and illustrates the appropriate text from *Exodus*, 2: 10. The composition is indebted to Poussin's *The Child Moses Treading on Pharaoh's Crown*.

231. COLUMBUS BREAKING THE EGG. April 1752. Etching. First state. $5\frac{5}{8} \times 7\frac{1}{8}$ ins. British Museum.

The subscription ticket to the *Analysis of Beauty*. Columbus wagered two critics of his discovery that they could not make an egg stand upright on the table until he showed them how. The story had been told earlier by Vasari of Brunelleschi, and before this by Luca Pacioli.

232. FRONTISPIECE TO 'THE ANALYSIS OF BEAUTY'. 1753. Size of engraving $2\frac{7}{16} \times 5\frac{1}{8}$ ins. British Museum.

Hogarth combines the serpentine line, a symbol of rococo art, with the ideal pyramid of the Renaissance. His quotation from Milton illustrates his favourite formal principle of rococo intricacy, which 'leads the eye and mind a wanton kind of chase'.

233. THE ANALYSIS OF BEAUTY. Plate I. March 1753. Etching and engraving. Third state. Signed. $14\frac{5}{8} \times 19\frac{5}{16}$ ins. British Museum.

The scene is a statuary's yard at Hyde Park Corner, and is based on the visit of Socrates to the yard of the sculptor Clito in Xenophon's *Memorabilia*.

Hogarth has here assembled the masterpieces of ancient sculpture known to the eighteenth century: the Farnese Hercules, the Vatican Antinous, the Laocoön, Venus de Medici, the Vatican torso by Apollonius son of Nestor, and the Apollo Belvedere. A dancing master rebukes Antinous for his slack and slovenly attitude.

The marginal figures illustrate passages in the text, notably his theory of the serpentine line or rococo line of grace which 'leads the eye and mind a wanton kind of chase'.

234. THE ANALYSIS OF BEAUTY. Plate II. March 1753. Etching and engraving. First state. Signed. $14\frac{9}{16} \times 19\frac{5}{8}$ ins. British Museum.

A ballroom scene, with a lover slipping a billet-doux to a young lady who is about to be taken home by her father, seen in the right-hand corner. Hogarth claimed that the hats could be associated with individual dancers.

The key to the meaning of the print is fig. 71 at the top right-hand corner. Hogarth believed that comic art required its own formal aesthetic, and that this should parody the forms of high art. The zig-zags, straight lines and geometrically bare shapes are therefore contrasted with the serpentine lines of the nobleman and his partner on the left.

In a later state the head of the nobleman was changed to resemble George III as Prince of Wales, one of several moves by Hogarth to enlist the support of the future King.

235. CROWNS, MITRES, MACES, ETC. March 1754. Etching. First state. Signed. Area of picture without inscription 5 × 7⅜ ins. British Museum.

An emblematical print on the patronage of the state under the King. The royal crown is shown as a sun shedding its rays upon the coronets of the House of Lords, the Lord Chancellor's Great Seal, the Speaker's hat, the Marshal of London's fur cap, the Cap of Liberty and the mitres and insignia of bishops, etc.

Characteristically, the patronage here celebrated is that of the Legislature itself, in passing the Copyright Act, also known as Hogarth's Act of 1735, protecting the right of artists and engravers to their own designs.

It was appropriately used as a subscription ticket to an election entertainment, an exposure of corrupt practices, it being Hogarth's practice to alternate satire on the bad with a eulogy of the good.

236. THE FRONTISPIECE TO 'KIRBY'S PERSPECTIVE'. February 1754. First state. Engraved by Luke Sullivan. Signed. 8³⁄₁₆ × 6¾ ins. British Museum.

Dr Brook Taylor's Method of Perspective was popularized by Hogarth's friend Joshua Kirby, who taught drawing to George III as Prince of Wales, in an edition of 1754.

The sheep getting larger as they walk into the distance, the old man on the hill lighting his pipe from the candle held out from the tavern window in the foreground, and the sportsman in a boat, who fires in the wrong direction at the gigantic cuckoo on a minute tree, provide the clue to a composition in which all lines lead to ludicrous conclusions.

237–40. FOUR PRINTS OF AN ELECTION. 1755/8. Etching and engraving. All signed. British Museum.

The election satire was occasioned by the Oxfordshire election of 1754. The four prints were dedicated respectively to Henry Fox, later Baron Holland; Sir Charles Hanbury Williams; Sir Edward Walpole; and George Hay, MP, the first three being prominent in the Whig party.

237. AN ELECTION ENTERTAINMENT. February 1755. Fourth state. By Hogarth, with assistance. 15⅞ × 21⁵⁄₁₆ ins.

Two Whig candidates for Parliament give a banquet to their supporters in the local inn while the rival Tory party parade outside the window. On this occasion there are no social distinctions between gentleman and voter, and alcohol has contributed to the general sense of equality.

At the left the first candidate, Sir Commodity Taxem, receives the confidences of a fat woman, a shoemaker pushes their heads closer together and turns his pipe out over the head of the knight, while a young girl admires his ring. In the next group a chimney sweep takes a similar opportunity to score off his social superior by squeezing painfully the hand of the second candidate in an affected demonstration of friendship and loyalty. A gluttonous clergyman acts as the division between these groups and the two succeeding ones, in which the gentry are successfully amusing their social inferiors. At the other end of the table the Mayor is being bled by a surgeon after a surfeit of oysters.

In front of the table a pedlar who has brought ribbons and knicknacks for sale as gifts looks with misgiving at a promissory note in lieu of cash. A butcher pours gin into the wound of a ruffian hired as bodyguard, and the election agent is knocked down by a brick hurled through the window. Notice that the bodyguard is receiving gin both internally and externally. Before the door a Methodist refuses to accept a bribe, while his infuriated wife points to the ragged condition of their son.

The inscriptions, slogans, etc., refer to the rival policies of the Whigs and Tories, the former advocating 'Liberty and Loyalty' and the latter 'Liberty and Property'. The Tories carry an effigy labelled 'No Jews' and oppose Excise Duty.

The scene is an illustration of the text, 'He that dippeth his hand with me in the dish, shall betray me' (*Matthew*, 26 : 23) and contains motives from the *Last Supper* of Leonardo da Vinci, although the composition is a parody of baroque banquet scenes.

238. CANVASSING FOR VOTES. February 1757. Fifth state. Engraved by C. Grignion. 15⅞ × 21¼ ins.

The iconographic reference is to *The Judgment of Hercules between Vice and Virtue*, i.e. Tory and Whig. The sly farmer in the centre is in the happy position of being offered bribes simultaneously by two innkeepers, whose services have been retained as local agents.

The inn at the left is the *Portobello*, representing the floating vote. A barber and a cobbler argue about the quarrelsome Admiral Vernon, who had brilliantly captured Portobello (1739) with six ships of the line, but failed disastrously to take Cartagena (1741). The inn on the right is *The Royal Oak*, the tree in which Charles II hid after the Battle of Worcester. Being a Tory inn, it displays a showcloth satirizing the Whig Duke of Newcastle as 'Punch Candidate for Guzzledown', shovelling out bribes. The view of the Horse Guards by Hogarth's *bête noire*, William Kent, shows an arch so low that the coachman's head has been knocked off.

The Tory candidate buys trinkets from a Jewish pedlar to secure the local influence of the two beauties on the balcony. The hostess counts her profits in a chair contemptuously made out of the British Lion, who has lost some of his teeth but nevertheless devours the French fleur-de-lis. A soldier of the English guards displays a keen interest divided between her purse and her person.

In the distance is the Crown Inn, belonging to the innkeeper on the left. A disloyal crowd assaults it beneath a sign-post which is being sawn down by a fanatic completely unaware that he is bringing about his own destruction as well as theirs.

239. THE POLLING. February 1758. Third state. Engraved by Hogarth and La Cave. $15\frac{15}{16} \times 21\frac{3}{8}$ ins.
Both parties have rallied every possible voter, even the disabled, lunatic and dying, and criminals temporarily released from gaol. The two candidates are seated at the back of the booth, with a sleeping beadle between them.
The lawyers of the opposing parties argue over the oath of the old soldier, who takes it with his hook instead of his right hand, the first declaring that it is invalid, the second protesting against so scandalous an injustice to a patriot wounded in the service of his country.
In the background Britannia's coach is about to be overturned while her coachman and footman play cards.

240. CHAIRING THE MEMBERS. January 1758. Third state. Engraved by Hogarth and F. Aviline. $15\frac{13}{16} \times 21\frac{7}{16}$ ins.
The two victorious Tory candidates are shown in triumphal procession, the shadow of the second being seen on the wall.
The central group is based on the *sacre conversazioni* of the Venetians and Rubens, the first Member of Parliament occupying the place of the Madonna on her throne. In accordance with Hogarth's theory of comic form and inversion of ideas, a zig-zag pattern substitutes the serpentine line of the baroque, bearers take the place of the attendant Saints, and a fiddler leads the procession, in lieu of angels playing music.
The dominant theme of the various episodes is imminent disaster. The bear leader is responsible for two. By fighting with a countryman armed with a flail he precipitates the rush of the sow, who has already overturned a woman and her litter of pigs into the stream. His neglected bear, prying into the pannier of the ragged man on a donkey, causes the gun on the monkey's back to be discharged in the direction of a chimney-sweep. A young lady behind the wall faints with alarm on seeing the danger of the Member, to whom she is related.
The defeated Whigs jeer at the procession from the house of a lawyer, who alone prospers from their humiliations. The house next to his is in ruins.
The famous Whig politician and humorist George Bubb Doddington, later Baron Melcombe, was the model for the elected Member. About his head flies a goose in parody of the eagle flying over the head of Alexander the Great in Pietro da Cortona's *Battle of Arbela*.

241. THE INVASION. Plate I. March 1756. Etching. Third state. Signed. $11\frac{1}{2} \times 14\frac{7}{8}$ ins. British Museum.
A group of thin French soldiers, one of whom is roasting frogs, prepare to embark for England in front of an inn with the sign 'Soup Meagre a la Sabot Royale'. Their banner is inscribed 'Vengeance et le Bon Bier et Bon Boeuf de Angleterre'. A monk examines a sledge containing instruments of execution and torture, and a 'Plan pour un Monastere dans Black Friars a Londre'.

242. THE INVASION. Plate II. Third state. Signed. $11\frac{5}{8} \times 14\frac{3}{4}$ ins. British Museum.
The corresponding scene in England. Outside the Inn of the Duke of Cumberland, hero of Culloden, a grenadier paints the King of France holding a gallows and saying 'You take a my fine Ships, you be de Pirate, you be de Teef, me send my grand Armies and hang you all, Marblu.' A girl measures the breadth of his shoulders, contrasting with the narrow round ones of the French. A sailor shouts 'Huzza' on a table with a copy of *Britannia Rules the Waves*. Such is the patriotism of the lad on the right that he stands on tip-toe to magnify his height in the hope of being accepted in spite of his youth.
Both these chauvinistic prints were prompted by the outbreak of the Seven Years War.

243. HOGARTH PAINTING THE COMIC MUSE. March 1758. Etching and engraving. The head only engraved by Hogarth. Third state. Signed. $14\frac{5}{8} \times 13\frac{5}{8}$ ins. British Museum.
On 16 July 1757 Hogarth was appointed Sergeant Painter to George II. The print celebrates his rise to the highest position open to an artist, and bases his claim to fame on *The Analysis of Beauty* and his genius as a comic history painter.

244. THE BENCH. September 1758. Etching and engraving. First state. Signed. $6\frac{1}{2} \times 7\frac{3}{4}$ ins. British Museum.
The Chief Justice is Sir John Willes, who allied learning with lechery, and next to him is Henry, afterwards Lord Chancellor and Earl Bathurst, shown sleeping.
The point of the print is indicated by the ironical dedication to George, later Marquis Townshend, who in 1756, with Matthew Darly, invented caricature in the sense of grotesque enlargement and distortion of salient features. Hogarth was strongly opposed to an innovation which he regarded as an attack on Nature and a denial of draughtsmanship. The aim of the satirist was to depict *character* and to find his models in the *outré* of Nature herself, exemplified by the comic but not exaggerated physiognomies of the Judges.

245. THE BENCH. 1758. Etching and engraving. Fourth state. $6\frac{3}{4} \times 7\frac{3}{8}$ ins. British Museum.
In this state Hogarth added at the top two profiles of the Lame Man in Raphael's *Sacrifice of Lystra* and a group of heads from Leonardo da Vinci's *Last Supper*, separated by two versions of his own sleeping judge. His object is to show that as the artist departs from nature by distortion, his drawing deteriorates.

246. THE COCKPIT. November 1759. Etching and engraving. Signed. $11\frac{11}{16} \times 14\frac{11}{16}$ in. British Museum.
The scene is the Royal Cockpit, Birdcage Walk, St James's Park. The central figure, modelled on Christ in Leonardo's *Last Supper*, is the blind Lord Albemarle Bertie, whose winnings are taken by a thief. The figures and episodes in the group on his left are symmetrically matched by those on his right.
In the foreground are two jockeys and a drunken man whose purse is removed by somebody's cane. A gallows has been chalked on a spectator's back.
In the gallery behind is a Frenchman wearing the Order of St Louis, immediately in front of the Royal Arms. The painting at the right depicts Nan Rawlings, a woman famous as a trainer of fighting cocks.
By the cockpit laws, a gambler who could not pay his debts was hoisted in a basket suspended from the ceiling. Its shadow falls on the arena, and reveals that the culprit is following the game and attempting to pledge his watch.

247–8. TWO ILLUSTRATIONS FOR 'TRISTRAM SHANDY' BY LAURENCE STERNE. 1760/1. Engraved by S. Ravenet after Hogarth. Both signed. British Museum.
Sterne had eulogized Hogarth in his novel, the first parts of which were published in 1760, and the illustrations were supplied for a second edition.

247. FRONTISPIECE TO 'TRISTRAM SHANDY', Vol. I. April 1760. First state. $5\frac{1}{4} \times 3\frac{1}{8}$ ins.
Corporal Trim reads the Sermon on Conscience to Dr Slop, who is asleep, Uncle Toby and Walter Shandy. On the wall are shown the fortifications of Namur.

247.*FRONTISPIECE TO 'TRISTRAM SHANDY', Vol. I. Drawing for the engraving, in reverse. Pen over pencil with additions in pencil. $5\frac{3}{8} \times 3\frac{1}{4}$ ins. New York Public Library.

248. THE BAPTISM OF TRISTRAM SHANDY, Vol. IV. January 1761. $5\frac{1}{4} \times 3$ ins.
Walter Shandy arrives too late to change the baptismal name of his son.

249. FRONTISPIECE TO JOSHUA KIRBY'S 'PERSPECTIVE OF ARCHITECTURE'. July 1760, published April 1761. Engraved by William Woollet after Hogarth. Signed. $9 \times 15\frac{1}{8}$ ins. British Museum.
The light of the rising sun's ray travels past a version of Bramante's Tempietto and a cherub reading *Palladio's Architecture*, to diagrammatic drawings and a model beneath a new Order invented by Hogarth out of the Prince of Wales' coronet and plume of feathers, and the star of St George. The landscape background is an imitation of Gaspard Poussin. The invention of new Orders was a favourite rococo pastime. The English Palladians had proposed a trinity of architectural heroes: Vitruvius, Palladio and Inigo Jones. The satirist wittily substitutes Bramante, Palladio and Hogarth.

250.*TIME SMOKING A PICTURE. Drawing for the engraving, in reverse. $9\frac{3}{4} \times 7\frac{1}{2}$ ins. Art Gallery of New South Wales, Sydney.

250. TIME SMOKING A PICTURE. March 1761. Etching and mezzotint. First state. $8 \times 6\frac{11}{16}$ ins. British Museum.
Intended as a subscription ticket for an engraving of *Sigismunda*. The Greek quotation from the Greek comic dramatist Crates has been amended by the addition of a negative to read: 'For Time is *not* a great artist, but weakens all he touches'. Hogarth is attacking the view of Addison (*Spectator*, No. 83) and the connoisseurs that Time mellowed paintings and improved them.

251. THE FIVE ORDERS OF PERIWIGS. November 1761. Etching. Second state. Signed. $10\frac{1}{2} \times 8\frac{5}{16}$ ins. British Museum.
A satire on phrenology and the cult of the Orders, occasioned by James Stuart's *The Antiquities of Athens*, the first volume of which had just been announced as shortly to be published.
Hogarth proposes five Orders: Episcopal (for Doric); Old Peerian or Aldermanic (for Tuscan); Lexonic (for Ionic); Queerinthian or Queue de Renard (for Corinthian); and Composite, or Half Natural (for Composite). A sixth order is added for the hairdressing of women.
The scheme is given as follows: A is the Foretop (Corona); B is the Caul (Architrave); C is the Friz (Frieze); D is the Necklock (Triglyph); E is the Buckle (Guttae); F is the Full Bottom (Base); G is the Aile de Pigeon; H is the Ribbon (Fillet); and I is the Curl (Volutes).
This scheme can be applied phrenologically. Thus the first Episcopal wig (Doric = Primitive) belongs to the head of Bishop William Warburton, the champion of Alexander Pope. The intellectual part (A) is very small; B is wide but shallow; C is big and bulky; G is protuberant and massive.

The head of Athenian Stuart is shown on the left, with his nose broken off to resemble a genuine antique. The first and only normal hairdress in the Order for Women belongs to Queen Charlotte.

252. ENTHUSIASM DELINEATED. *c.* 1761. Etching and engraving. $12\frac{5}{8} \times 14$ ins. British Museum.
A satire on Methodism and Old Masters, dedicated to the Archbishop of Canterbury, but never published.
The preacher, modelled on George Whitefield, has a harlequin's robe under his gown and the tonsure of a Jesuit under his wig, thus equating Methodists and Catholics according to a popular prejudice of the time. He holds two puppets: the first, God with angels from the Stanza d'Eliodoro in the Vatican, the second, a Devil holding a gridiron. Other puppets, Adam and Eve, Peter with his key pulling Paul's hair, Moses and Aaron, await their turn.
The text of the sermon is 'I speak as a Fool' (*2 Corinthians*, 11: 23). A thermometer in place of an hour-glass gives the key to the reactions of the congregation, ranging from Luke Warm to Convulsion Fits, Madness and Despair. Prominent among the congregation are Mother Douglas, the pious bawd, having convulsion fits, and a Jew in the manner of Rembrandt, with his Bible open at the Sacrifice of Isaac.
At the window a Mohammedan Turk is amazed to see such strange manifestations of Christian piety.

253. CREDULITY, SUPERSTITION AND FANATICISM. April 1762. Etching and engraving. Second state. Signed. $14\frac{1}{2} \times 12\frac{5}{8}$ ins. British Museum.
The changes reveal why Hogarth never published the preceding print. He has eliminated the satire on famous religious paintings and images which might give offence, including the image of Christ.
Mother Douglas has been replaced by Mary Tofts, who claimed to have given birth to rabbits (No. 112). A witch on a broomstick is substituted for the Trinity, and an altar with a bloody knife takes the place of the Sacrifice of Isaac. Most of the congregation now refer to notorious cases of delusion and imposture, and there are several allusions to the Cock Lane Ghost whose image appears above the thermometer.

254. FRONTISPIECE TO THE CATALOGUE OF THE EXHIBITION OF THE SOCIETY OF ARTISTS AT SPRING GARDENS. May 1761. Etching and engraving by C. Grignion. Third state of the first version. Signed. $6\frac{7}{8} \times 5\frac{3}{8}$ ins. British Museum.
Britannia in the rôle of Grammatica waters the flourishing saplings of painting, sculpture and architecture from the fountain that gushes from the lion's head beneath the bust of the new king, George III.
The exhibition, promoted by Hogarth, was a landmark in the history of English art and led to the foundation of the Royal Academy.

255. TAILPIECE TO THE CATALOGUE. Engraved by C. Grignion. First version. $4\frac{1}{2} \times 5\frac{1}{8}$ ins. British Museum.
The one-eyed monkey is a connoisseur watching three withered exotics, labelled 'Obit 1502', 'Obit 1600' and 'Obit 1604'. The dates, which presumably refer to the invasion of England by foreign art, have never been satisfactorily explained.

256. SIGISMUNDA. *c.* 1760. Etching by James Basire. Signed. $12\frac{11}{16} \times 14\frac{3}{16}$ ins. British Museum.
The painting was a commission from Sir Richard Grosvenor, who refused to pay the price. Hogarth wished to rival a version of the same subject, reputedly by Correggio, but really by Francesco Furini.

257. THE TIMES. Plate I. September 1762. Etching and engraving. First state. Signed. $8\frac{9}{16} \times 11\frac{5}{8}$ ins. British Museum.
An attempt to support the unpopular Ministry of the Earl of Bute, the Scottish favourite of George III, against the warlike policy of William Pitt.
A fireman from the Union office (referring to the Union between England and Scotland) is trying to put out the fire which threatens to burn the English half of the globe. He is opposed by rival firemen from the Temple Coffee House, named after Pitt's brother-in-law and champion, Earl Temple. The Pitt faction are busy setting up their signboards in opposition on the other side of the street to the burning house of the Prime Minister: the *Patriot Arms*, in which patriots are divided against themselves; the *Newcastle Inn*, which is also the Post Office for the Duke of Newcastle's vast correspondence about bribery and office-seeking: the *Norfolk Jig*, referring to the Norfolk Militia, then the most regimented of the nationalist volunteer corps; and *Alive from America*, alluding to the visit by Cherokee chiefs, exploited by City merchants in their drive for imperial expansion. Henry VIII fanning the fire with his bellows is a hit at the tyrannical and overbearing conduct of Pitt himself.

258. THE TIMES. Plate I. Etching and engraving. Third state. Signed. $8\frac{9}{16} \times 11\frac{5}{8}$ ins. British Museum.
Pitt now takes the place of Henry VIII, probably because the original allusion was too subtle and far-fetched.

259. THE TIMES. Plate II. 1762 or 1763. Etching and engraving. First state. Signed in later states. $9\frac{1}{8} \times 11\frac{7}{8}$ ins. British Museum.
The garden of good government is watered by the pump of royal patronage worked by Lord Bute (left) and issuing from the lion's head beneath the statue of George III, copied from the portrait by his former Sergeant Painter Allan

Ramsay. On the left the royal garden is inspected by the combined House of Commons and House of Lords. The Lords are in various states of lethargy and indifference, while in the Commons, separated by a railing, Pitt and others fire at the dove of peace in the sky.

On the right crippled veterans of the Seven Years War try to gain access to the royal island by a bridge which has been blocked off. Before them an abusive mob gathers round Mrs Fanny (the impostor of the Cock Lane Ghost fraud) and John Wilkes in the pillory, his pockets turned out in allusion to his debts.

Hogarth has included in his satire an attack on the Society for the Encouragement of Arts, shown in front of St Mary-le-Strand, because he disagreed with its policy of awarding premiums.

260. DR THOMAS MORELL. February 1762. Etching by James Basire. Third state. Signed. $7\frac{11}{16} \times 5\frac{13}{16}$ ins. British Museum.
The frontispiece to the Greek *Thesaurus* published by the scholar, a close friend of Hogarth, in 1762.

261. FRONTISS-PISS. 1763. Etching by La Cave. Signed. $5\frac{1}{2} \times 3\frac{1}{4}$ ins. Royal Library, Windsor Castle.
An illustration to an unpublished pamphlet by Dr Gregory Sharpe, a chaplain to George III, attacking the aesthetic theories of Frances Hutcheson.

The water of nonsense pours down from an old witch seated on the moon of madness. The mice are the followers of Hutcheson, who have been killed by reading his book and are now washed away by the final deluge from the author, now dead and transformed into a witch. Those who are alive attack the telescope and works of Newton, the apostle of sense.

262. HENRY FIELDING. April 1762. Etching and engraving by James Basire. Second state. Signed. $7\frac{1}{8} \times 4\frac{1}{2}$ ins. British Museum.
The only authentic portrait of Fielding, drawn by Hogarth from memory eight years after his death for *The Works of Henry Fielding*, edited by Arthur Murphy, 1762.

263. JOHN WILKES. May 1763. Etching. First state. Signed. $12\frac{1}{2} \times 8\frac{3}{4}$ ins. British Museum.
On May 6 John Wilkes was brought before Chief Justice Pratt, later Lord Camden, at Westminster (where Hogarth sketched him), on a charge of sedition, but was discharged. He is shown holding the Staff of Maintenance surmounted by the Cap of Liberty. Full justice is done to his squint, and his wig is curled to resemble Satanic horns. Beside him are *North Briton 17* and *North Briton 45*, the numbers in which he attacked Hogarth and George III respectively.

263.*JOHN WILKES. Drawing for the engraving, in reverse. Pen and brown ink over pencil; incised. $14 \times 8\frac{1}{2}$ ins. British Museum.

264. THE BRUISER. August 1763. Etching and engraving. Second state. Signed. $13\frac{1}{2} \times 10\frac{5}{16}$ ins. British Museum.
The Reverend Charles Churchill, in defence of Wilkes, had attacked the artist venomously in 'An Epistle to Mr Hogarth'. This is Hogarth's reply.

The print is a reworking of the artist's self-portrait (see No. 218). The clergyman is depicted as a hard-drinking, bullying bear clasping a club with knots inscribed 'Lye 1', 'Lye 2', etc. Hogarth's dog Trump is shown expressing his opinion of Churchill's *Epistle*. The books refer to the *North Briton* and the debts of Wilkes. The Line of Beauty has been removed from the palette, which is now blank. If the Wilkes faction come to power, the future of art is doomed.

265. FRONTISPIECE TO 'PHYSIOGNOMY' BY THE REV. JOHN CLUBBE. December 1763. Possibly engraved by Luke Sullivan. $8\frac{5}{8} \times 7\frac{1}{8}$ ins. British Museum.
An illustration to a satire on phrenology in the manner of Swift. The specific test is for measuring the gravity of heads by a weighing machine. The stages are: A, absolute Gravity; B, Conatus or exertion against absolute Gravity; C, partial Gravity; D, comparative Gravity; E, Horizontal, or good Sense; F, Wit; G, comparative Levity, or Coxcomb; H, partial Levity, or pert Fool; I, absolute Levity, or Stark Fool.

Hogarth may have chosen this particular passage in the text because it corresponded to his own theory in *The Analysis of Beauty*, where he related deformity to extremes.

266. THE FARMER'S RETURN. March 1762. Etching by James Basire. Second state. Signed. $6\frac{7}{8} \times 6$ ins. British Museum.
The frontispiece to the comic interlude by David Garrick, published in 1762. The farmer, who had been to London for the coronation of George III, frightens his household by telling the story of the Cock Lane Ghost.

267. TAILPIECE, OR THE BATHOS. April 1764. Etching and engraving. Signed. $10\frac{3}{4} \times 12\frac{13}{16}$ ins. British Museum.
This is Hogarth's final testament, wittily based on Dürer's *Melancolia* and Salvator Rosa's *Democritus*, and intended to serve as a tail-piece to a complete set of his engraved works. He was adding finishing touches to it only a few days before he died.

Time expires against a ruined column. His scythe, hour-glass and pipe are all broken. With his last breath he utters 'FINIS'. His right hand still clutches his last Will and Testament, bequeathing 'all and every Atom thereof to Chaos whom I appoint my sole Executor. Witness Clotho. Lachesis. Atropos.'

Below him in the foreground are scattered the emblems of extinction: a play opened at its last page and 'Exeunt Omnes'; an empty purse; the discarded last of a shoemaker with its waxed 'lead'; a broken bow, unstrung; a worn-out wig-brush with no bristles left; a fragment of a crown; a rope-end; the butt-end of a musket; and the stump of a broom.

Above, in the sky, Apollo lies dead in his chariot led by lifeless horses; the sun is in eclipse. A ship lies wrecked in the motionless sea, and a pirate hangs from a gallows on the sea coast. The church tower is ruined, and the dial of the clock has lost its hands. The tombstone retains the skull and bones, but has lost its inscription. On the right the oak is blasted, its last gesture one of menace to Apollo. The inn is roofless, and its sign 'The World's End', the globe in flames, is shown toppling. The bell of the church tower is cracked; in its fall it has joined a smashed flagon of gin. In the text below, the two quotations from Tacitus and Maximus Tyrius support the argument of the *Analysis of Beauty*, the emblems of which are depicted in the flanking medallions. Hogarth ended his career as he had begun it, with a satire on the connoisseurs, but this time he proclaims the enduring value of art and the aesthetic values on which it is based.